W9-CHS-092

Susan,
Hope you
enjoy reading
my little Book! I to
Feel free to email
call or email
anytime
chat!

Dr. Deb
& Grezie

5/02

Seeing
Eye to Eye
With Your Dog

Solving the Canine Puzzle

by Debra Schneider

Copyright © 1999 by Debra Schneider

Printed by Banta Information Services
7000 Washington Ave S.
 Eden Prairie, Mn 55344
(612) 826-3500

Editing and Design by Anne Kilgore

Marketing and Advertising: Michele Klecker
MK Ads, P.O. Box 22
River Falls, WI 54022
(715)-426-5024

Front Page photograph by Michael G. Schneider

All rights reserved. No part of this book may be
reproduced by any mechanical, photographic or
electronic process, or in the form of phonographic
recording. Nor may it be stored in a retrieval
system, without permission from the Author.

Library of Congress Cataloging-in-Publication
Data

Schneider, Debra
        Seeing Eye to Eye with your Dog, Solving
        the Canine Puzzle.
        ISBN #0-9676315-0-5

*This book is dedicated to my husband, Michael,
and my children, Adam and Jacob.
A special thank you to my first basset Kelsey,
who taught me how to be the trainer I am today,
And to all my friends, both two leggers and four,
whose constant inspiration kept me going!*

Kelsey, C.D., CGC 1985 - 1998

Contents

Seeing Eye to Eye With Your Dog
Solving the Canine Puzzle

contents

contents

Introduction

This book is the first of a series of three that I intend to write. This first book is on communication between dogs and humans. The following book will be on training and the third will be focused on beyond the training years.

I wrote this book for many reasons. I wrote it for all the frustrated dogs whose owners just don't understand. I wrote it for the owners who, after their couch is chewed up, look at their dogs and say "what were you thinking!" This book is written from a dog's point of view. Communication is the key to solving the canine puzzle. Unfortunately when it comes to the human/canine relationship, we speak different languages, thus the difficulties begin. I have seen training methods which include screaming NO at your dog and rushing at them when they make a mistake. I have seen dogs lifted off their front feet by their leash and collar and jerked back and forth for an inappropriate behavior. I have seen dogs wearing shock collars because they bark too much, or are aggressive. I'm saddened for both the owners and the dogs that violence seems to be the only way they feel they can communicate with each other. Please don't misunderstand me, I can be very firm with my dogs when I need to be, but I'm fair about it. Coming from an abusive and severely controlling relationship in my past really opened my eyes to the harshness of force training. I know I didn't do very well with it, and neither will your dog.

In my profession I have the challenge of helping folks understand why their dogs do what they do. I also reap the rewards of seeing dog and owner find a comfortable and acceptable relationship as each discovers how the other works. It doesn't take my students long to realize that the class is really for the human, and that both of them will be learning. Most often you will read books on how to train your dog. In this book you will see how our dogs clearly tell us what works and what doesn't, and how to work our training into these behaviors. Resistance is a form of communication and by ignoring what our dogs are trying to tell us, we start the tug-of-war of the species!

It is my hope this book gives you cause to say "hmmmm, never thought of that before." If that happens, even once, then I've accomplished my goal. It's my belief that training should fit both the dog and the trainer. Training a dog can be a bit like dancing. You must both find the same beat if you're going make it work!

I've had the good fortune of having hundreds of dogs "talk" to me as they go through my classes. My students have often heard me say "you know, if I was your dog....." As you train, take a moment to think from your dog's point of view. Pause for a moment and look into those wonderfully bright and warm eyes of your canine friend. Soon, the puzzle will be solved and the two of you will be seeing "eye to eye!!"

Best woofgards and good reading!
Debra Schneider

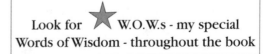

Look for ★ W.O.W.s - my special
Words of Wisdom - throughout the book

1

Is there place in our lives for a dog?

When considering dog ownership, most folks think only about whether or not they want a dog. Seldom do they question, is there a place for a dog in our lives? In my profession I've spent many hours consulting with people on the responsibility of dog ownership. Finding the right breed to fit the family is second to the question above. Owning a dog takes money, time, training, and most importantly, accepting a dog for what it is, a dog!

In order to help folks answer those important questions, I've put together a questionnaire for my clients to fill out. Once it's finished, we get together and chat about dog ownership and breed types. In the questionnaire there are points where if you answer yes or no, you will be told to stop, that getting a dog isn't in everyone's best interest at this time.

How expensive is this puppy?

I have the privilege of working closely with Dr. Kate An Hunter, DVM, who owns Carver Lake Veterinary Center in Woodbury, Minnesota. Recently she put together a list of expenses that would have to be paid out during the first year of a dog's life. This list included first year puppy shots, spaying or neutering, limited toys and books, food for an average (30-40 pound) dog, training classes (puppy kindergarten and beginner), and a miscellaneous column which included leashes, collars, bowls and treats. The first year costs came to $1,000. That did not include the price of the puppy; and don't forget unexpected expenses. There can be that emergency surgery because your dog ate the remote control. Are you in the position to pay $1,000 for surgery on one hip that is dysplastic? These are serious issues that should be considered. It's a sad day for everyone when a dog has to be put down because the owner couldn't afford the surgery. Better to think ahead now so that you don't have to be put in that heartbreaking position.

Another dollar amount often overlooked is the damage a puppy can do to your house. I read a recent study which showed that the average puppy can do up to $1800 of damage in a house during the first year alone. If you've owned a dog before, you know how easily this happens. A shoe chewed, a favorite belt destroyed, the carpet piece that needed to be replaced, your daughter's favorite beanie baby, the corner of the wall that was redecorated and the attraction of those infamous remote controls.   The list is endless. I always remind my students in Puppy Kindergarten class to expect to lose something to those sharp little puppy teeth. No matter how well you puppy proof your home, there is always that one time they find something we hadn't thought of!

Let's not forget the cost of grooming. If you have decided on a dog that needs to be groomed in order to look like the breed, expect to pay anywhere between $20-60 every 4 - 6 weeks, depending on the requirements of the breed. We sometimes forget when looking at pictures that cute appearance takes grooming, and that they don't typically come that way!

Do I have the time?

There isn't any way around it, dogs take time. If you are already busy with kids' functions or a tight work schedule, it may be that a dog simply wouldn't fit at this time in your life. I'm a firm believer that a dog should be part of the family. This means he isn't left outside in a kennel all day and all night. A dog should be able to go to places with his family (when it's appropriate!). These are social animals. They do not do well left alone for extended periods of time.

Dogs also need exercise. Exercise is not a casual walk around the lake. Dogs need to be tired out. My motto is "A tired dog is a good dog!" The dog's breed and preferences will determine how much and what kind of exercise they will need. Even the smallest of dogs needs a chance to burn off energy. Being loose in a fenced in back yard does not constitute exercise. Seldom do you see a dog come in from the back yard with his tongue hanging out, flopping himself down on the floor to rest!

Often folks will ask if they should get two dogs to have each other for company. Having two is perfectly all right as long as you have the time to spend with both of them. If not, the end result will be that you have two dogs that are extremely bonded with each other, and not as strongly bonded to you. Establishing leadership can be a bit tricky when the dogs have one another to fall back on. That special bond that we all want with our dogs does not come free. We must work at it, build it, and nurture it. Owning multiple dogs means double the work. Owning three dogs myself means that I must split my time three ways. Each dog needs their special time with me, be it a walk alone, time in the yard playing fetch, training time, or just sitting in front of the TV being groomed and fussed over. We also spend time as a pack, out in the yard while they watch me work (they're very good at that) or in the house hanging out. I suggest getting one dog at a time, and add them when YOU want another dog, not when you think your dog needs a pet.

Having a dog does not mean that you delegate the responsibility to a child. If a dog is coming into a household, there should be an adult ready and willing to do much of the work. Children can most certainly help with the care, as it teaches them many things. But as we all know, kids will be kids, and dogs can sometimes be left in the wings when new activities come along. Never do I encourage a family to purchase a dog solely to have for the kids. I've heard too many stories of dogs tied up in the back yard and ignored, while the adult stands firm saying "this dog wasn't my idea," or worse, "it's not my responsibility to take care of it." Who suffers here? Only the dog. So please, take a moment to consider the time involved with a dog. It simply isn't fair to purchase a dog and then after six months discover you can't find the time for him. This is far too common a reason why dogs are surrendered at our local shelter. The "disposable dog syndrome" is filling our humane societies with dogs faster than we can find homes for them.

No, he won't outgrow that!

Training is the most essential part of owning a dog. They do not come to us pre-programmed to be the well mannered dogs we envisioned when we adopted them. It's our responsibility to shape them, teach them and mold the behaviors we find acceptable. Training should start the moment the puppy comes into your home. Rules should be set before you bring home a puppy, so that everyone in the household understands what the puppy will and won't be allowed to do. Home schooling can work, but isn't always com-

pletely successful. Going to a class will help discipline you to work with your dog every day. As a professional trainer I know I can train my dogs at home with a fair amount of success. Still, I opt to participate in classes. It helps my dog learn to work with different distractions, off his home turf. If my dog will do a sit stay in the ring with 10 other dogs, there is a good chance I can replicate that behavior out in the real world. It's also good to have another pair of eyes looking at the two of you work. As owners we tend to ignore some of the behaviors our dogs throw out. For example, I had a student whose dog constantly whined in class. He never corrected it, and never seemed to acknowledge it was going on. The rest of the class would give him the "can't you do something" looks, but he was oblivious. After class one day I asked him, "doesn't the whining get to you?" He answered, "what whining?" We then learned that this dog has whined since the day he was brought home, and the owner had learned to tune it out. Another great example of how our dogs can train us!   Looking at this, a person could say, "If it doesn't bother the owner, why should we care?"   Well, it did bother the owner, but he didn't know how to correct it, so he opted to ignore it. Many dog owners will accept a bad behavior, not because it doesn't bother them, but because they don't know how to cope with it.

Training is an essential part of owning a dog. Without training, the human/canine relationship can be very strained and unrewarding.

Accept him for what he is!

Dogs are carnivores. They have teeth that can hurt. They eat just about anything they can get their mouths on. They bark, they defecate in your yard and your house. They shed their hair on your couch, your chairs, and clothes. Short hairs get caught in the weave of furniture and stay in it forever!   Long hair can gather together to form balls of fuzz under chairs and in corners (dog owners affectionately call these "dust bunnies"). Some breeds have their own special odor, for example, my bassets share a unique "hound scent" that they carry in the oil of their coats. You can't miss it, especially when it settles in your car on a hot day! Be prepared for your dog to smell like a dog.

Dogs destroy things. They love to chew, rip, shred and tear. They especially love items that have your scent on it, including your underwear, socks, or shoes. You must dog proof your house to protect things of value to you. Long tails can knock off a pretty vase in one swoop. Little dogs can jump up on tables in a single bound, scratching woodwork as they go.

Dogs tie you down. When you travel, you must always decide what to do with the dog. Can he come with? Will Aunt Alice let

Fluffy into her home for a week? Will a friend take him, or will you kennel him. My Board and Train program is full of dogs whose owners have taken trips and thought it would be a good time for Fluffy to go to "boot camp!" This adds to the cost of a trip.

Dogs dig, and dig, and dig. Some dig for the pure joy of it, some try to get those pesky rabbits out from under your porch. Some dig so they can lie in the hole they've dug. They like the fact that you fill up the hole they've just dug because now they can dig another! Dogs can be great gardeners. As Dr. Hunter put is so well one day, "they see you dig a hole, so they dig a hole, they see you dig a hole, so they dig another!"

Dogs bark...loudly! Depending on the breed, some can be more vocal than others. This is one of their forms of communication and although we can curb it, we can never make it go away completely, nor should we try to. Dogs bark when they're happy, sad, bored, excited, afraid, aggressive, or just to burn off some energy. Modifying this behavior can take time and training.

Owning a dog is a legal liability. The law states we must have our dogs in control at all times. This means that if your dog snaps at, bites, or injures another human or dog you are liable. Aggression can be perceived differently by different people. A simple growl can be a very fearful thing for a non-dog person. Be prepared to be responsible for every action your dog takes.

So why would I include such negative things about owning a dog? Because this is the nitty gritty of living with a canine. It's the every day challenge of things you simply can't change or train that can wear on an unprepared owner.

I tell all my friends that my house is dog friendly. It gives me a great excuse when my house is a bit messy and company stops by! Love me, love my dog is a motto well used here at the Schneider home. All the things my dogs do because they're canine, I accept, and you must too if you're going to own one. Yes, you can look for the breeds that shed less, but he's still going to do everything else on the list. You can find a dog that is less vocal and may not bark as much, but he will still do dog things. For many people, their house is their showcase. I respect and actually envy those people. If you have a house where you feel the dog can only be in one small area, you may want to rethink owning a dog. Dogs love to be with us, hanging around with the pack. I'm not saying you should let your dog run amuck throughout the house, but be sure he can be in areas where you spend the most time.

So if all of the above is acceptable, then it's time for you to have a dog. The relationship between our two species is an interesting, challenging and rewarding one. Life is good when you can come home from a long day at work and are met at the door by a dog that is always happy to see you, no matter what mood you're in. Unconditional love is the biggest reward we reap from our dogs. They give that to us, even when we may not deserve it.

Take a moment to read and answer the questionnaire on the next page. It may help you make that final decision on "Do I have a place for a dog in my life."

WOW: Getting a dog should not be a spur of the moment decision. Buying a puppy as a gift is never a good idea. Although your heart may be in the right place, choosing a puppy should be a personal , planned choice. It may be that they weren't ready for this living gift or the time may just be wrong. Always choose your own dog as an individual or family. If everyone in the family wants the dog, it's sure to be a win/win situation!

CHOOSING A DOG TO FIT YOUR LIFESTYLE!

Choosing a dog takes time, consideration, thoughtful analysis of breed type and temperament and most of all, commitment.

The questions below will help you through this process. At certain points, depending on your answers, the questionnaire may tell you to stop, that owning a dog isn't in your best interest at this time. These questions were compiled from the web page of ARPO (Advocacy for Responsible Pet Ownership), Firstline Magazine, including Dr. Kate An Hunter and my own thoughts based on our experiences with our clients.

Thank you for taking this first responsible step!

The Family Meeting:
1. It is important that <u>every adult</u> in this family wants this pet. If someone has concerns, or says they don't care, it won't be their responsibility, then the answer to owning a dog is NO. YES____ NO____

2. *Expenses:* Owning a dog is a financial commitment as well as an emotional one. Can the family budget afford the health care, training, food, treats and general maintenance that this dog will cost? YES____ NO____. If the answer is NO, then stop here.

3. *The Primary Care Taker:* The primary caretaker must be an adult. Children can most certainly help, but should not be considered the Primary Caretaker. Is there an adult to assume this responsibility? YES____ NO____ If the answer is NO, then stop here.

4. *Where will the dog be kept?* It is important everyone agrees as to where the dog can live, i.e., in the house, outside. Also, where will the dog be allowed to live within the house? If a family member objects to having a dog in the house, then stop here.

Dog Ownership History:
1. Have you owned a dog before? Yes_____ No_____
   If yes, for how long?_____
2. What type(s) of dog did you own before?

   _____

3. What did you like the most about the dog?

   _____

   _____

4. What did you like least about the dog?

   _____

   _____

5. Do you still own the dog?   Yes____ No____
   If no, what happened to this
   dog?_____

Personal Information:
1. What best describes your lifestyle? Very Active____ Active_____
   Not very Active_____   Inactive_____
2. What best describes your personality?   Firm____ Tolerant_____
   Soft_____ Lenient_____
3. How would other household member's personalities affect pet
   ownership?_____

Home and Household Information:
1. How many children in your home? ____What are the ages?____
2. What type of home do you live in? _____
3. Do you live in the : City_____   Country_____ Suburb_____
4. What size yard do you have? Small_____ Medium_____
   Large_____
5. Is your yard fenced? Yes____ No____
6. Where will your dog sleep at night?

   _____

7. Where will you keep the dog when you're gone?

   _____

8. How will you confine your dog (either inside or out?)

   _____

Dog/Breed considerations
1. How regularly will your dog be exercised?
_____

2. How much time can you spend grooming?
_____

3. Which size appeals to you most? Small dog_____
    Medium dog_____ Large dog_____
4. Which coat type appeals to you most? Short_____
    Medium_____ Long_____
5. Would you consider a rescue or shelter dog ? Yes_____ No_____
6. Would you consider an adult dog? Yes___ No___

Expectations
1. Are you planning on using this dog for its particular breed
    purpose (ie, hunting, herding) Yes _____ No _____
2. If you could have the perfect dog, what characteristics would it
    have_____
3. What physical characterstics would your perfect dog have?
_____

Five Tough Questions: Ask yourself and your family these five
questions before you decide to own a dog.

1. Are you ready to make a long-term commitment?
2. Does everyone in the family want to adopt a pet?
3. Who will be the primary adult caretaker?
4. Can you afford this animal?
5. Are you committed to making this animal a good citizen by
    training it to be a welcome pet in public parks, on walks and as a
    visitor? (Research shows that people who take the time to train
    their dogs are likely to keep them longer than people who
    don't.)

Choosing your Dog

By going through your answers you can now start the process of finding your breed of dog that would best fit your lifestyle. It's important that you not only look through books and do research, but also call the local clubs in the area, talk to your veterinarian, some breeders and call a dog trainer. These resources will help you pinpoint the dog that will best fit you. The more you can learn about the breed you are interested in, the better prepared you will be when you have the puppy living with you. Look for the best and the worst in the breed you are considering.

Do your homework by making a list of Pros and Cons on your particular breed. After you've done all of this, it's time to find the pup! When looking, only work with reputable breeders. Stay away from the back yard breeder who sells his puppies in the newspaper like a used car. A reputable breeder may cost more, but you are getting years of good breeding, a contract to protect both you and the breeder, and a wonderful resource to depend on when odd things come up with the pup.

Don't forget to check your local shelters as well. Adult dogs are very often gems in disguise!

2

We're getting a dog!!

So it's a go! The decision has been made and you're ready to find the perfect dog for you. By this time you should have done your homework and decided on a breed. Homework on breed selection includes reading every thing you can get your hands on about the breed. You should have talked to your veterinarian, asking about potential health risks associated with this breed. You should have talked to your local trainer or behaviorist, asking about possible special training needs. You may have decided to go to your local shelter and adopt a puppy or grown dog.

Purchasing a Purebred Dog

If you've decided to purchase a purebred, then the next step will be to find a reputable breeder. This is the most crucial decision you will have in finding your perfect dog. Whomever you choose will be your best resource to answer any future questions you may have about your breed. Finding a breeder takes time and patience on your part.

The Reputable Breeder: To find a reputable breeder you may have to do a little leg work. Get in touch with your vet, ask your local training school, get on the internet and talk to your local breed club for names. The reputable breeder is one that is active with their breed. They may show them in conformation, obedience, tracking, or hunting. They live with this breed, and have proven dogs with titles. Titling a dog takes time, patience and money. It also proves that this dog is all they say it is, because it has been tested or examined by experts who agree. Often I'll hear folks tell me, "but I don't want a show dog, I just want a pet." A litter of six puppies may have only one or two show quality puppies. The rest are pet quality. This simply means they may have too much leg for the breed or not the right tail set. The faults are minor and not important to a pet owner. So purchasing a pet quality puppy ensures you the good breeding and upbringing a show quality puppy would get, but usually at a lower price.

A good breeder will ask you a lot of questions before they ever agree to sell you a puppy. They may have you fill out a questionnaire. Don't be surprised by this, as they are simply making sure that this is the breed for you and that the puppy will fill all your expectations. You may be a bit put off by this, but remember, they have the dog and your best interest at heart. Many times you will find a waiting list for an upcoming litter. A reputable breeder will usually have two or three puppies already sold before they breed the dog.

A reputable breeder will sell their puppies under contract. This contract will depict the dog as either pet or show quality, and the price and wording of the contract will reflect this. The reputable breeder will want to be the first person you contact if you can't keep your dog. The contract will state this. She may want the dog back, or be willing to help you find a good home. There may be limited health guarantees on breed specific problems, e.g. hips or eyes.

You will pay more for a puppy from a breeder, but will pay less in medical problems in the long run. There are many genetically passed medical problems in the dog world. A reputable breeder will not breed a dog that has a known medical issue. Genetically passed problems can include hip dysplasia, thyroid problems, heart diseases, hearing loss or eye problems. The list is a long one; be sure you know your breed's specific medical concerns.

And finally, the reputable breeder will be your best resource to turn to when you're having problems with your dog. They know this breed inside and out. They may have had the same problem with Dad or Mom. When you purchase a puppy from them, they may very well have picked it for you. They know their puppies' personalities to a tee, and are in the best position to pick the puppy that fits your personality and lifestyle.

Avoid: Uneducated breeders, those that are breeding just once. Don't purchase a puppy from someone who hasn't raised it themselves. And remember, AKC* papers only ensure that the dog is purebred, it does not make it an exceptional dog.

Finding a mixed-breed

Finding the right mixed breed puppy can be a bit more challenging. If it's a puppy, there is no guarantee on its size as an adult. If it's a lab/shepherd mix, you cannot know if it will want to swim and retrieve or herd your kids! The notion that "mixed breeds are not as nervous and high strung" is simply not true. Mixed breeds can have all the good or bad traits of the breeds they share. You never know what you're getting. I've heard many a student tell me "yep, they said this dog wouldn't get over 20 pounds, and look at the 65 pound moose now!"

Don't forget, there are plenty of puppies as well as adult dogs, both purebred and mixed, sitting in the local shelters hoping for a home.

Choosing and buying the puppy

Before you buy the puppy, there are a couple of things to check out first.

1. When you first go to look at a puppy, leave your children and your checkbook at home! That way you can go home and make the right decision without those bright little puppy eyes begging you to "take me!" This decision will affect you for many years, so

don't buy a puppy out of pity or impulse.

2. Was the puppy raised in a household environment? If not, leave that puppy behind and find another. Human socialization is so very important, and the first 9 weeks of life are crucial for the puppy to bond and accept humans as part of their pack.

3. DO NOT take the puppy home before it is 8 weeks or older. Puppies learn a lot about being dogs during the time of 4-10 weeks. They play dominance games, and learn bite inhibition. Without bite inhibition, you will have a puppy that doesn't understand that it's wrong if he bites too hard. It makes for a tough time training. I personally like to see them stay a few weeks longer. Never take a puppy that is six weeks or younger, as trouble will follow, something we'll be talking more about later in this book.

4. Was the environment clean from feces and urine? Housebreaking goes much easier when a puppy has been kept in a clean environment and didn't have to sit in feces. I remember feeling like the "poop queen" while raising up my six basset hound babies. I was always begging for old newspaper from my friends. A puppy that has lived in a dirty environment won't care if he piddles in his crate and has to sit in it. He's used to it and has grown up with it. With my puppies, I brought in two small crates and placed them inside the exercise pen (which was in a room off of the kitchen). I left the doors off so they could crawl inside whenever they wanted to sleep. It made crate training a snap for my puppy owners because these little guys already had it figured

out that kennels were great to sleep in, and not a place to get dirty. So check out what kind of environment they were raised in, as you will have to work with the impact it has left on your puppy.

5. If you are a first time dog owner, do not take two puppies from the same litter. Normally, the breeder will not sell you two puppies, as they are aware of the sibling puppy syndrome. This is where the littermates bond strongly with each other and not as strongly with the human. I see them come into my school on occasion, and it's always a challenge trying to train them separately. They do not do well if they aren't together. One may cry or simply shut down, or be very distracted looking for the other. Take one puppy, and later down the road, add another if you want two. Besides, there is plenty of work with just one during that first year.

6. Choosing your puppy: Do not be offended if your purebred breeder chooses the puppy for you. As I said above, they know their puppies' personalities, and can, from your answers to their questions, make a fairly reliable match. They may offer you two puppies with similar personalities to choose from. If you are in a position to pick from the litter, be sure you're choosing the puppy that seems to be the "middle of the pack" kind of puppy. Don't choose the one that hides and seems sad. Future behavioral problems could develop with the shy puppy. The "in your face" kind of puppy may be more of a challenge than you are ready for, depending on what you are going to be doing with him. I encourage folks to pick the puppy that is interested in you, friendly and happy. He's the guy or girl that may get pushed a bit by other littermates, but definitely isn't the bottom of the pack.

7. Gender: *Male or Female?* Typically I tell people not to choose between sexes, but rather choose the puppy that best fits them. The difference in temperaments can vary breed by breed. When

choosing, don't get caught in the trap of putting human emotions on the different sexes. Female dogs are not more maternal and loving. That's a human trait we've affixed to them. Males can be stereotyped as pushy and rowdy leg lifters. So pay more attention to the personality of the puppy you're looking at and less to the gender.

8. Temperament traits can be passed on, so be sure to see Mom, and Dad if he's available. Are they friendly? Are there any signs of shyness or fear? Although you may not see these traits in the puppy now, as he grows they could develop. From my own experience, I've lived with a well bred, but shy dog. We've worked very hard on helping her learn appropriate "stress busters" (which for her is a down stay). As a professional trainer I have done everything right with her, but her shyness is a personality trait I've had to live with. We've been able to manage it, but never eliminate it. In this case, both Mom and Dad were fine, so even with all the odds in her favor, she still came "hard wired" this way. So if Mom or Dad don't seem right to you, find another puppy.

9. In the first chapter we talked about accepting a dog for what he is. There was also a questionnaire to fill out. In the questionnaire it asks about your personality traits. When looking for a puppy, we're most often happiest when we find a dog that shares our own approach to life. For example, I personally like ones that have a sense of humor about life. My two bassets, Gus and Maybee, definitely have that. Their motto "don't get stressed, just get silly" fits my way of thinking just fine! Now this could very well drive a logical, serious minded person crazy. Know that breed types can have tendencies towards certain traits, although again, it's never a guarantee.

Choosing a Veterinarian

Choose a Veterinarian <u>before</u> you bring your puppy home. I encourage my clients to interview, talk to and visit potential veterinarians so that when the puppy comes home you are not in a rush to get to the closest one. Your vet should be someone you feel comfortable with. You may want to ask them what pets they have, have they shown or bred dogs, do they have a special area of expertise. Check out the facility, is it clean, are the folks at the front desk pleasant and helpful. What other services do they offer, for example, grooming or dog training. Do they have up-to-date equipment, for example, an ultrasonic dental scaler. Can they monitor the pet while it's under anesthesia. Remember, you get what you pay for, so bargain shopping isn't always the best way to choose a veterinarian. Let your gut tell you how you feel about the place. If you're bringing in an adult dog, set up a simple nail trim and get a feel for how the doctor interacts with you and your dog. Does your dog like the veterinarian? You may have to depend on these people to save your animal's life some day, so choose carefully.

*AKC - stands for American Kennel Club. Purebred dogs who are registered with this club will have registration papers. Let it be known that having a dog with AKC papers does not make it more valuable or special. Oftentimes people will try to use this as a selling tool. Papers simply mean the dog is registered as a purebred. When purchasing a purebred dog, you most certainly should get papers on it.

WOW: Finding the perfect dog for you and your family takes time. Be prepared to take months before you have a puppy. Breeders waiting lists can be long, so get on more than one. Doing your homework on the breed before you decide will pave the way for a wonderful match. Also, if you've decided on a breed, be sure you've personally met more than just one of the breed of your choice. Too often I've heard of folks who have gotten a dog because they know one and think it's wonderful. The more you meet the better feel you will have for their good as well as not so good points.

3

Getting to know you

So you have the new puppy or dog home. Now it's time to get to know each other. The first two weeks you spend with your dog are critical, as it lays the groundwork for your future relationship. That's why it's so important to have the rules established <u>before</u> the dog comes into your home. Letting him get away with inappropriate behaviors because "he's just a puppy" or "he's just getting settled," gives the dog the wrong message. He won't stop biting or jumping on your counters after he's been with you longer, and there are very few behaviors he will outgrow. Start getting to know your dog as soon as he comes into your home.

Understanding your dog's hard wiring as well as his personality will benefit you greatly as you build your relationship with him.

Hard Wiring

Hard wiring describes traits you cannot change in your dog. They come wired this way because of their breeding and the fact that they are canine. It's important to know what drives a dog to do what he does. With this information you can then modify and shape his behaviors in a way that will satisfy both your wants and his needs.

Canine pack behavior ...who's the leader? Dogs are pack animals. They understand and follow social hierarchy. This means they will come into your home looking to see where they fit in. They start this the moment they are introduced into the family.

They already fought for and established a hierarchy within the litter. Every day the litter would ensue on another battle to see who would be king of the hill for that particular moment. I remember watching my six puppies wrestle, bite and snarl with each other over toys, bones and rights to sleeping quarters. It became clear as the weeks went by which puppy fell where in the pack. Each went home with a personality description, including where I felt  this puppy fell on the dominance ladder. These puppies took their basic traits with them into their new homes. Riley, who tried to be boss at all times with his littermates, has always been a challenge to his owners, Kerrie and Jon. During his first year with them he tried to bully his way around, just as he did with his littermates. Because he had owners, and a breeder, who understood his "wanna be leader" attitude, we could work with it. If we hadn't understood, he might have been labeled a bad dog. Both his owners and myself have called him many names, but never a bad dog. He simply pushes all the rules all the time. These are things we cannot change with our dogs, but we can manage with the right understanding.

Establishing a leadership role with your dog is your first step towards a harmonious relationship. In my seminars I have participants list briefly, using their own personal experiences, traits and skills of both the best manager they ever had and those of the "not so great" manager. Typically, the lists looks like this:

Good Manager:
Strong communication - clear goals
Immediate reinforcement
Allowed to make a mistake and learn from it
Never screamed or yelled
Trust

Encouragement
Supportive
Team Player
FUN!

Poor Manager:
No trust
Temper
Moody
Inconsistent
Condescending
Lack of Leadership
Made work drudgery
No clear goals

Note that all the traits of the good manager can be applied to a good dog owner. If, within a department, there is lack of leadership you often find groups that are struggling to be productive. Instead of working as a team towards a goal, there are often internal conflicts. If the boss doesn't seem to want to be boss, a person who isn't the boss tries to do the job but, isn't very good at it either. If, within your home, you don't make it clear to your dog that you are the boss, he may feel he has to take over that role. Dogs tend to make pretty lousy leaders in the human world. Most really don't want the role, but because it's being forced on them, will find a way to handle it, and it's almost always done with inappropriate behavior. It may show up as a dog being aggressive or shy. He may bark or lunge at the perceived foe. While this is going on, the typical owner will be left wondering how to handle their aggressive dog, when all along the aggression was really a leadership problem. Dogs are wired to respond to leadership as well as lack of leadership.

We send many invisible messages to our dogs when we allow them to do things that we see as sweet or cute but they see as getting their way. In the dog's eyes, **leaders always:**

choose their place of rest. Since you sleep in the bed, it must be the best place, so if they can sleep in the bed, guess you're equal for the night! Also, the couch or chair is a great place and if we can share it, then again, we're equal! If you do allow the dog up on the furniture, my advice is be sure they're only coming up on invitation. In other words, they shouldn't be jumping up on their own accord. Make them sit, and then clearly give them an okay and pat on the couch. That way, it's under your command that he's there.

initiate the play by tossing the ball. Ever get one plopped in your lap by your dog? Demanding when to play and when not to, like the dog that only retrieves twice then drops the ball and walks away, is a leaders choice. It should always be your decision, never the dogs, to play. This doesn't mean if your dog asks that you can't respond, but I tell my students to ignore that ball placed in their lap, and then a minute or so later discover it, and act like you just had the best idea. Look at the dog, smile and say "do you want to play?" This, in a fair and easy fashion, clearly tells that dog that you are in control. The game becomes even more fun when the leader starts it!

go through doors first. I've seen this with my dogs over and over. I know exactly out of the three who will get out first. It hasn't changed in a long time. Teaching your dog to wait at the door until you go through or give the okay to go out could save his life, and also sends a mini message that you're the leader, he's not.

eat first. If you free feed your dog, you're missing out on an easy way to exhibit leadership. The leader eats first, and then the others can eat. By feeding your dog after you've had breakfast and/or supper, he clearly understands that he's not the leader today. How many times have you watched documentaries on wolves and seen them feed. The alpha pair always gets to eat first, while the others beg in the background (sound familiar?). If someone tries to sneak a bite, the alphas will chase him off and keep him away until they're done. Once the alphas are finished, the rest come in to feed, in accordance to their rank in the pack.

walk in a straight line. Everyone gets out of his way. Always make your dog move for you if he's in your way. This is not to say you must always be giving your pup the boot (in a kind way of course, no kicking the dog!), but it wouldn't hurt to make a big show of moving him up from a favorite sleeping spot just because you wanted to make a point. He shouldn't have any qualms about moving for you. Just as he should move off the couch easily if you tell him so.

I've had the pleasure of working with folks and watching the relationship between the dog and human change drastically over a period of time because of simple changes in how the two interact. Dogs spend a lot of time watching our every move. If a change in the family occurs, for example, someone leaves or moves in, often the dog goes through an adjustment period as he works out how this change effects his place in the pack. Just like people, some will adjust more quickly than others. Always remember your dog's world is his pack. He's not worried about the interest rates or how Dow Jones did that day. He's interested in whether or not you'll forget and let him get up on the bed tonight. He is always testing, waiting to see if you might just slip up a little.

Communication

Dogs have a completely different form of communication than we do. They talk mostly with their body posture and eye contact. High pitched tones generally mean food and excitement to them, while lower tones can mean aggression or dominance. Many of my female clients complain that the dog listens much better to their husbands than to them. Is the husband a better trainer? Not necessarily, but he may have deeper resonance to his voice in which the dog is responding to. Dogs also tend to get very excited around children, not only because they move quickly and are at the dog's level, but because they have high pitched voices that tell the dog fun is to be had!

Breed Specific Behaviors

If you've done your homework on your breed, then these behaviors will not be a surprise. For example, herding dogs, like border collies, were bred to work all day. Their energy level is endless. The instinct to keep things together can be overwhelming to a dog that is living in a family unit. If the dog isn't given a channel or outlet for these instincts, he will find his own way to satisfy them. That's when I hear complaints like, "he is nipping at the children when they run," or "he won't leave the cats alone!" These dogs also use their eyes to hold and move the livestock. This means they stare, and since there aren't any sheep, you may find your border collie spending a lot of time looking in your face. This can be a bit scary to the person who thinks the dog is trying to be dominant by always looking into their eyes, when he's really just acting on breed instincts.

Labradors are wonderful dogs, but again, they were bred for endurance in the field. Our black lab Tucker could work all day in the field looking for pheasants. During the 9 months of the year when he couldn't hunt we had to give him at least two to three runs a week in the field or he started all kinds of naughty behaviors. Labradors are also very oral dogs. By this I mean they love to have things in their mouths. If a toy isn't available, your hand will work just fine! Play mouthing is a common complaint of my sporting dog owners. Understanding this potential problem (and remember, all dogs are different, so it can be that not every Labrador or Border Collie will have these traits) will help to channel the behavior. When Tucker played with any of the family members, he would run and get a toy in his mouth. We taught him that this was an acceptable behavior, and it also filled his need for oral satisfaction. It made us all happy!

Personality

The best thing about your dog will be his own unique personality. Learning his likes, his dislikes, what motivates him or turns him off will be the biggest step in communicating with him. In my years of training I've never seen a dog that was just like another. They may look physically alike, but there are always differences in how they act and respond. For folks that are replacing a passed on senior dog with a new puppy, this can be a hard thing to remember. Often, when talking about their new puppy they will say "Senior never did what Junior is doing!" or "Senior just learned all this on his own, we never had to take him to class." Some of these things may be true, but I will say this, that life has a way of softening our memories of our past loved pets. If Senior was 15 years old when he passed, that means it has been a long time since Senior was a puppy. We tend to forget the woes and troubles Senior may have caused long ago. Your own lifestyle is also bound to be different. Children may be part of your life now, or they may have moved out. Always remember every dog has his own way of coming at life. It's unfair to think Junior can or will replace Senior. He won't. But he will fill your life in a new and wonderful way for sure!

Naming the Puppy

The name of your dog reflects a lot about you and your family. How the dog was named is a very important piece of information for me, as a trainer and behaviorist, as it tells me how involved family members were in this important part of the puppy process. Dogs that are named by children, without the parents input, are ones that were bought for the kids, and the parents are just the pocket book. Dogs that were named by the children, with the help of their parents show that the entire family is interested in this puppy.

If the adult named the dog, I will ask them how they came up with the name. I hear many interesting reasons, most common is that the name shows strength, softness or reminds them of a childhood dog .

If you're not sure what to name your dog, take three or four possible names and run them by the dog. For example, when we fostered a five month old springer spaniel, he came to us with the name Winston. He had been a stray, and the shelter folks had given him that name. He didn't know it, so we decided to change it. When I said the word "Flint," he came right over wagging his tail. He named himself. So Flint he is to this very day, and he loves his name, no doubt about it!

Take the time to name your puppy well. Remember, you have to live with this name for many years to come, so it should be one that you, and your dog, like and are comfortable with.

If you have an older dog that came with a name, change it. I strongly suggest this whenever a client adopts a dog that already has a name. Give this dog a clean slate to start with. We don't know how his name was used in his past life, or what he connects with it. So give him a brand new name that you can give the meaning of love and care to!

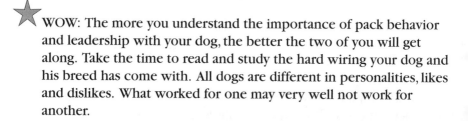

WOW: The more you understand the importance of pack behavior and leadership with your dog, the better the two of you will get along. Take the time to read and study the hard wiring your dog and his breed has come with. All dogs are different in personalities, likes and dislikes. What worked for one may very well not work for another.

4

Rules for the First Two Weeks

Whether you have puppy, an adolescent or adult dog coming into your home, the first two weeks can be very important in how your dog will look at your relationship in the future.

We call this period the "honeymoon period." For the first couple of weeks everyone is excited to have the new puppy or dog around. Everything they do wrong is excused because "after all, it's just a puppy," or "he's still getting used to things here. He didn't really mean to snap at me!" If only folks would be proactive in training, meaning they begin working on a problem before it even starts, I believe I would have fewer students in my classes. Jumping, barking and pulling on a leash are the main complaints from most of my students. You'll read over and over in this book, "dogs will do what works." Teach them from day one what you expect and you'll be a proactive trainer instead of a reactive one!

RULES:

Consider for a moment how dogs get to know each other and how quickly they understand each other's personalities. If a new dog is introduced into the house, he is quickly sized up by the other(s). There is little tolerance for unruly behavior, i.e., snapping or growling. Dogs will either retaliate or leave if this happens. When a new dog comes into the home, it's best to start laying down the rules immediately. Make it clear to the dog what is expected, and be fair about it. Being fair means being consistent. For example, if Mom says the dog can't be in the living room, but Dad sneaks it in when she's away, a mixed message is being sent to the puppy. Remember that dogs see things in black or white; either they can or they can't, it's safe or it's dangerous. So the puppy allowed to come in the living room by Dad will assume it's always okay. He'll be confused when Mom's anger is misdirected at him when he happily walks in there. Typically, the puppy takes the blame of being naughty and will probably be corrected. Was it really the puppy's fault? Of course not, he was just doing what he had been allowed to do on other occasions. When we aren't consistent with the rules, the dog will choose the one that he likes best, which typically isn't the right one!

I encourage folks to list out the rules for the puppy. If there is more than one person in the family, including children, be sure that everyone has read the rules, or listened to and understands them. I advise my clients to make rules for the children in regard to what they can and cannot do with the puppy. This may include not running when the puppy is out or always playing quietly when the puppy is with them. If a child breaks the rule and the puppy acts inappropriately, both need a time out. Too often dogs and puppies are accidentally set up to fail. A fast moving child is a pretty hard temptation to resist so when the puppy chases the child, perhaps nipping at sneakers as they go, whose fault is it? Actually, it's everyone's. It's the parent's fault for not supervising interaction between the child and the puppy. It's the child's for breaking the rule and running, and it's the puppy's for acting inappropriately with his mouth. When training or shaping a behavior, we must look at our own actions before deciding that the dog can't learn!

QUIET CONTROL:

Previous experience teaches puppies how to interact. For example, the child that inter- acts with the puppy by running, jumping or playing tug of war will have a harder time interacting with the dog on a quieter level. The dog is always going to try to entice the child to play in the expected mode. I hear many stories about dogs using their teeth, in play, with the children but never the parents. One theory is that in a dog's mind, children are littermates, thus explaining the wild play.

I personally have a hard time believing that. I know my children have grown up with dogs, but they sure don't look like or act like dogs! In defense of the puppy, he is simply acting on a learned behavior. If typically the child plays chase games, we can't expect the puppy to know when he can chase and when he can't. He has learned to respond in a certain way to the child, and will continue to do so until taught otherwise.

I encourage children to play quietly with the puppy. If they are younger than ten, they should always be supervised until the puppy has grown and proper behaviors have been established. Include the children in the training of the puppy. This will set the stage for the dog as he grows. His learned behavior will be to respond to all members of his pack. Play should always be initiated by the pack members and ended by the pack members. Clearly tell the puppy that play is done either by walking away or dropping the toy and saying "enough." Appropriate play needs to be taught. It's when we assume that our puppy or dog understands how to play with humans that we set the puppy up for failure. Puppies know how to play with each other, but again, they learned that from their littermates. He didn't come into your house understanding human play. All the more reason to understand the importance of teaching proper play with humans.

If the puppy is going to be out in public, or guests are coming over, a leash will go a long way in helping the puppy learn how to interact appropriately with strangers. If you don't want your puppy to jump on your guests, you must start modifying that behavior from the first day he enters your home. Remember that dogs will do what works. In other words, if he has spent the last month jumping on people and being responded to, he will continue it. You should start immediately by teaching him the sit command. Always have the leash on when people come over so you can help him learn by having him sit before anyone says hello to him. If you don't have a leash on him, the control will be harder, and the message may come across differently than you wanted. A puppy that has learned to sit for attention will take this behavior into adulthood. With consistency you will have a dog that greets strangers and guests by sitting quietly, as he has learned that this will give him the greatest reward, attention!

WHAT TO FEED HIM:

When I was growing up, there really weren't any choices in dog food. All the dogs ate the same thing. The new age of health awareness has affected not only human, but canine consumption as well. We now have numerous foods to choose from. If purchasing a puppy from a breeder, they will often give you a starter bag of food. Our clinic gives a free bag of food with every first well puppy visit. The choices can be overwhelming. My feeling is to start out with the food the dog was eating before he came to you and make a change only if you or your veterinarian consider it warranted. Unlike humans, dogs do not get bored with their food. I have yet to see my dogs turn to me and say "kibble again?" I do, on occasion, supplement their food using healthy choices. You should talk to your breeder and veterinarian about appropriate supplements to your dog's diet.

There are a few things to keep in mind when choosing a food. Many premium foods may cost more, but you feed your dog less of them. Be aware that the feeding instructions on the back of the bags are typically on the high end, so you should talk to your breeder or veterinarian about the right amount for your dog.

Dogs often defecate less on the premium foods (less volume in, less volume out), which is a big plus when you realize instead of 3-4 defecations a day, your dog is only doing two. Some foods are preservative free, but this means they have a shorter shelf life, so be sure to check the expiration date.

If you are going to change your dog's diet, do it slowly over a 3-4 week period. This way you can watch and make sure that your dog is tolerating the new food and not having any adverse reactions. Speaking from experience, I once changed my border collie's food. I started out putting just a small amount of the new food into her old. Within a week of eating just a small portion of the new food, she started to itch, badly. I pulled her off the food and she improved immediately. I can only imagine what she would have gone through had I not taken it slowly and instead given her a full bowl of this food. Your dog is not a human, and shouldn't be expected to handle sudden changes in their main based food from day to day as we do.

Another hot topic is whether or not we should feed "people food." I don't consider any meat people food. I consider it dog food, since canines are carnivores. Vegetables and fruit are not people food either, as many other animals and birds eat them. These foods, in the right increments, are good for your dog. Basically, if it's good for you, there is a good chance it's good for your dog. Ice cream, candy, cookies and the such, are considered people food and should be avoided when feeding your dog.

FEEDING SCHEDULE:

The feeding schedule should be one that works around your lifestyle. The key is to keep your dog on a schedule. Leaving down food sends the wrong message to your dog. Making sure your dog knows that food comes from you is important in his assessment of your value to him. He needs to know that you, the leader, supply the food. It just doesn't appear out of nowhere. Scheduled feedings will ensure that you know when he's eaten and how much. It will also help out immensely with housebreaking as dogs that eat on a schedule will eliminate on a fairly consistent schedule. Fresh water should be available at all times unless you are working on a housebreaking problem.

Various factors come into play on how often a dog should be fed. Puppies need to be fed 2-3 times a day until they are 4 months old. Then two times a day. After a dog is 8-10 months old, feeding may drop to once a day. I like to see my students feed their dogs twice a day, if scheduling allows. A dog that is fed twice a day may be less anxious about eating, thus may eat slower (although I must say, my lab, Tucker, never did realize this!), which is healthier for them. It may also cause less stress about needing to guard their food. No matter when you feed, it's safe to say your dog will tell you when it's time to eat. I am always amazed at how my dogs can tell time, although they are responding to their body's clock, not mine!

TREATS:

Be sure to watch how many treats you are giving your dog. Rewarding them for doing nothing but looking cute can cause a finicky eater and a dog that thinks, "why should I sit on command for a cookie when I'll get one later?" Make them earn those goodies every time by having them sit or lay down, or simply settle next to you. We call this N.F.F., nothing for free. Imagine you were paid for staying home. How many of us would still say, "no, I must go to work!" Treats are your dog's paycheck. Make him earn them and he'll respond better to you!

CONFINEMENT/SLEEP AREA:

Be sure you've decided where the dog should sleep. A crate or wire kennel should be used with puppies and new dogs for the first few months. This secures the dog and keeps him safe while you sleep. The kennel can be in the bedroom with you or in the family room. Do not put the crate down in the basement or out in the garage. Dogs are pack animals and there is nothing more stressful or depressing for a dog than to know that the pack is "in there" and "I'm out here." Be sure you're also putting your dog into his crate while you are home so he can have naps and quiet time. If the crate is only used for separation, when you leave or go to bed, you will have a dog that doesn't appreciate his "den" and may have issues about going into it. Crates are wonderful tools if not abused. A puppy (2-4 months) shouldn't be left in a crate for more than four hours without a break. Until a dog is six months old, I encourage folks to go home during lunch to let their dogs out for a stretch, or get a neighbor to help. An adult dog can be in his crate during a normal 8 hour work day.

Remember, freedom is a privelege that must be earned. Don't be in a hurry to let your dog loose in your house until you're sure he can be trusted.

IDENTIFYING:

You must put a collar and some form of identification on your dog as soon as he enters your home. A simple tag with a phone number is all that is needed. Just this morning as I was writing this book, I looked out the window and saw a very nice, well taken care of dog wander into the neighbors yard. I went out to see if she had a tag on her collar. She was happy to come over and say hello, but there was not a tag to be found on her. Usually I would keep the dog and call animal control, but in this case I was not at my own house. Because I didn't know the dogs around the neighborhood I simply told her to "go home." She slowly turned and walked away. I can only hope she went home. If she had been tagged, I would have gladly returned her.

The importance of identifying your dog, whether they are house dogs or not is seen at our shelter every day. Numerous dogs are dropped off that were found wandering the neighborhoods without identification. Remember, it only takes one time for your dog to wander through an open gate for you to lose them. Don't risk it, tag them the moment they are yours.

There are other forms of identification as well. Microchipping is growing in popularity. This small chip is inserted with a syringe, by your veterinarian, inbetween the dog's shoulder blades , just like a shot. The chip has a number that can be read with a scanner that all police, shelters, vets and humane societies have. You are given a small yellow tag with an 800 number on it and also the number of the chip. The number is for the national registry. The registry will call you and pass on the information about your dog's whereabouts. This protects your personal information, i.e., your home phone number and address.

So be sure to identify them immediately. Don't forget, if your dog is over six months old, most cities require he be licensed. Check your local ordinances to find out what your city requires.

EXERCISE AREA:

Be sure you've decided where your dog will be allowed to relieve himself. It's our job to teach the puppy or dog where it's appropriate. If you want him to go in a certain place in your yard (and this makes clean up a lot easier!), then you'll have to start now, by taking him out on leash to the same place. Put a word to it, so your dog will start to put together that when you say "hurry up" or "do your business" that he needs to get busy and not dawdle. If, after he's done, you want to take the leash off so he can have time in the yard, feel free, but tell him to "go play!"

CAR RIDING:
    Now is the time to decide where your dog should ride when he goes out with you. We'll be talking more about car training later in the Life Saving Skills chapter.

WOW: Setting some basic rules down for your dog as soon as he arrives will help everyone get into the groove of living with a canine. Your dog is only trained in canine manners, so it's up to you to help him understand his new role as a member of a human pack. Our cultures are very different, and your dog has a lot to learn. Don't send the wrong messages early on in the relationship and then blame the dog as he grows but still exhibits his puppy behavior.

"Teach me more!"

5

Simple training starts now!

Training can be started as soon as your puppy enters your home. Learning from you is a skill he must practice. Think of the following tools as a seam in a dress. It's not the entire garment, but without it there would be a definite hole!

CONNECTION WORD - your invisible leash:
Decide on a word you will be using with your dog that will mark the desired behavior. Consider this the opposite of the NO command, which is what we use to mark negative behavior. Typically we use the words nice, yes, good, excellent. My students have become very creative in their connections words. I've heard words like wow, yeah, A+, cute and super. These words are said with lots of enthusiasm. General praise, like good dog, are not considered connection words because we use them often during the day (I'm always cooing to my dogs and telling them they're good dogs!). This word will also help you teach your dog a solid recall.

NAME GAME:
Teaching your new puppy or dog his name should be easy, but we sometimes unintentionally put a negative meaning onto it. For instance, it's very easy to say the dogs name and No, i.e., Fluffy, NO! In Fluffy's mind, you said his name, he looked at you or responded in some way, and then you said NO. A smart dog may very well say "that sound ain't so great, why should I look when I hear it?" No certainly has a place in a dog's vocabulary, but never attached to his name.
The first exercise my puppy kindergarten or beginner students teach their dog is the name game. It's important, for a couple reasons, that the dog always look at you when you say his name. First, a dog that isn't looking at you will most likely not respond to your command. He's simply not connected to you at that moment. Second, it's crucial if your dog is running away. If you can't get him to stop and look at you, you're not going to get him back by yelling come. The name game also teaches the dog that his name is the greatest! Food is always a part of this exercise - you say his name, when he looks, he gets praise and a treat.

CRATE TRAINING:

Crates are a very natural way to contain your dog when you are not home, or when you are home and you need your dog to be out from under your feet! Start them out now, and remember, it's called training, which means you have to teach your puppy or dog to enjoy his crate. Students often tell me that their dog doesn't like the crate, so they stopped using it. This is but the first in a number of challenges you will have training your dog. By giving up, your dog has learned that this method of resistance worked for him, so he may very well try it with other training sessions.

A crate is a den for your dog. Dogs will naturally find places that remind them of dens (under your bed, under the porch, behind your couch). If trained properly, your dog will enjoy having a place of his own, where he can get away from the buzz of a busy family or simply a place to take a nap.

To properly crate train your dog you should start on a weekend, when you have time to be putting him in and out on a regular basis.

1. Begin by feeding your dog his meals in his crate with the door open.
2. Put his toys in the crate so he has to go in to get them out
3. Sit on the floor and lure him in with food (toss it in so he goes into the crate). Have a treat ready when he turns to come out so he's getting one with his head towards the door.
4. Eventually he will go into the crate looking for the treat - have one ready when he turns around to leave the crate and reinforce his being in the crate!
5. Purchase a Kong and put some peanut butter or treats into it.
6. Place it into the crate with your dog. Shut the door. Let the dog out before he's finished with his Kong. Put the Kong up.

Repeat number six, each time leaving him in a little longer.

In order for a crate to be comfortable, your dog should be able to stand up and turn around in it. It doesn't have to be huge, but he shouldn't be cramped. The crate should be in a place where the family is (the family room, kitchen or living room). Some people find it handy to have two crates, one in the living area, and one in the bedroom. Remember, a dog is a pack animal, and will not take kindly to being shut away in the basement or laundry room. Letting a dog sleep in your room is an easy way to have quality time with him. He'll feel better being close to you and you may get a better night's sleep!

Do not leave your dog in a crate for more than 8 hours (a normal workday). Do not put the dog crate by a window so your dog can look out! It's very frustrating for a dog to see things and not be able to get to them. Better that he sleeps away the day while you're gone!

Use the crate when you're home. If you only use the crate for separation (when you leave or go to bed) your dog will not like being there. Help him to understand that the crate is his place, and that he can be in it even when you're home. A good time to crate your dog is while you are eating. Also helps with the begging problem!

A dog must EARN the privilege of being loose. You may find that it will take years before you can trust your dog loose in your house. Some will never earn it. It all depends on the dog. A crate keeps your dog safe while you're gone. It's also a wonderful way to travel with your dog, as it ensures his safety in case of an accident or if you have to make a very fast stop.

Take your time with crate training. Some dogs will take to it easily - others may have some issues with it.

Housebreaking the Adult Dog

Adult dogs who defecate or urinate in the house do so for many reasons.

*   They are intact males or females who are marking their territory
*   They may have medical reasons (e.g. a urinary track infection)
*   They never had to hold their urine, thus the muscles were never developed
*   They were raised in a dirty situation, and are used to living in

their own feces
- They are exhibiting signs of separation anxiety or stress

Once you pinpointed the reason for your dog's problem, the training can be much easier.

Intact animals spend alot of time marking. They will mark in your house, on your furniture, on your clothes. Get this dog altered as soon as possible! Sometimes a male neutered later in life (beyond a year old) will require more training time because he has learned this behavior versus the younger male who is marking out of instinct and is just beginning this behavior.

A dog that is urinating frequently may very well have an infection or medical problem. Be sure to bring your dog in to see your veterinarian before you decide that it's a behavioral problem.

Dogs that were never housebroken never had to hold it. Housebreaking is a brain game as well as a physical ability. He must want to keep his area clean, but he also must work his muscles. Using a crate (see Crating your Dog) will help him learn to use these muscles appropriately.

The dog raised in a dirty environment is the hardest dog to housebreak. If he has been forced to live in his own feces for a long time, then he hasn't learned to keep his area clean. This means he will mess in his crate as well as your house. This dog needs to be watched constantly, perhaps even brought to a doggie daycare while you're at work, to help him learn to be clean.

Dogs will defecate out of stress. If you find that your dog is messing in the house when you're gone, this may be a result of separation anxiety.

Housebreaking an adult dog is not unlike housebreaking a puppy. It includes feeding on a schedule, using a crate, and constant monitoring. Remember, a dog must EARN the right to be loose in your house. Crating is a fair and reasonable way to manage the housebreaking problems you may be experiencing with your dog.

Housebreaking a Puppy:

Using your crate, a feeding schedule and supervision will help ease this process along! Puppies who are given too much of the two Fs (freedom and food) can be harder. Housebreaking is not only a physical effort on your puppy's part (he has to learn to hold it, and that means strengthening and learning how to control the muscles), but also a brain game, meaning he must learn what you want as well. He needs to be crated until he is fully housebroken (no accidents for two full months) and has earned the privilege of being loose in your house.

A couple of easy rules to follow:

1. Keep your puppy on a leash when you take them outside to go potty (this tells them that they have something to do, otherwise they will ramble around and take their time).
2. Decide on a word for the action (outside, hurry up) and use it as your dog is sniffing around. This helps your dog learn to eliminate on command.
3. Be sure you've got a schedule set up for your dog, for example:

> 6:30 - puppy gets up, comes out of crate and goes outside
> 6:45 - puppy is fed
> 7:00 - puppy is taken outside
> 7:15 - puppy plays
> 8:30 - puppy is taken outside
> 9:00 - puppy is put back into crate for nap

The schedule can be the same for noon, afternoon and evening. Feeding on a schedule and letting them out every 1/2 hour (on leash!) when not crated will help with housebreaking.
4. If the puppy does make a mess, clean up with white vinegar and water.
5. USE A CRATE! Puppy should be crated during the day for a few hours, even if you're home, and at night. If puppy is messing in the crate, remove the bedding, or make the crate smaller.
6. If you know it's time for the puppy to eliminate, but he won't go,

put him back into his crate for 20 minutes and try again later (this eliminates the opportunity for puppy to go off into another room to do his business).

7. Make sure to get the puppy out after 15 minutes or so of hard play. Nature dictates that the more he moves, the more he needs to eliminate!

8. SUPERVISE, SUPERVISE, SUPERVISE! If you can't watch your puppy every minute, then put him in his crate. The fewer opportunities he has to eliminate in your house, the quicker he will learn.

9. Be outside with your puppy watching him eliminate. Just because he spent 30 minutes out wandering around does not mean he did his business! It's also a great chance to train him to go to one spot.

10. Feed on a schedule so you know when it's gone in, as it will need to come out within 30-40 minutes!

11. Lastly, don't physically correct him if you catch him in the act. Tell him, NO, outside, pick him up and take him out. Do not rub his face in it or use a paper on him. This can create the "hide it" puppy. A smart puppy will think that since you seem to have a problem when he goes in front of you, he will go in another room where you can't see him.

SUBMISSIVE URINATION:

   This can happen when a young puppy meets someone new, or a member of the family comes home and greets the puppy. Don't correct for this - it's not a housebreaking problem. Your puppy will outgrow this. If it is a big problem, then simply have your company ignore the puppy for the first 10 minutes until he settles down.

SHARING:

   Puppies need to learn from day one that you may take whatever you want from them, but that you will always give them something back. This should start with the food bowl. I know many folks will pick up the puppy's food bowl, pretend to eat, or look at it, then give it back. This is fine until the day he gets old enough to say, "hey, that's mine you can't have it!" I encourage folks to play the swap game. If I take something from you, I give you something in return. In regards to the bowl, when you go down to put your hand into the bowl, do so to put a really good treat into it. Have your children do the same. The puppy then learns that if someone messes with his bowl it's a good thing, something great will be dropped in. You can also take the bowl, put in a special treat, and put it back down. Bowl guarding can be a nasty behavior that will manifest itself into a bite someday if not "nipped" in the bud from the get go.

I also teach that if you take something from a puppy, like your sock, that you give him back something of his, like his chew toy. It clearly tells the puppy that "no, you may not have that, but you can have this." That goes along with the alternate behavior approach. Don't just say no and grab. You'll teach your puppy behaviors that will not be appreciated when they grow up and run away with your belongings!

TRAINING CLASSES:

Get your puppy signed up for a Puppy Kindergarten class as soon as you can! This is the opportune time to teach your pup - when he's young and doesn't have any ingrained or learned behaviors yet. Puppy Kindergarten is typically for puppies between 2-4 months. Now is the time to start building the framework of your future relationship.

SOCIALIZATION:

It's important to acclimate your puppy to as many new things in life as you can. Keeping him cloistered in your house, even if you have kids coming and going, will not help him become socially balanced. He must be brought out and about, after he's had his first set of puppy shots. Take him with you to your friends house or go to the pet store and let people see him. Teach him that people come in many shapes, sizes and colors, and that they are all perfectly okay. What happens often is, at first the puppy is a novelty and it's fun to take him over to meet Grandpa or to a friends house. After 3-4 weeks, everyone has seen him, so the puppy doesn't get out and about. Socialization is an ongoing process, one that is most important during the first year. Don't make the mistake of thinking because you have a busy household and the dog sees children or adults coming and going, that this will fulfill his social academics. It is most certainly good for him, but doesn't complete the requirements. He must be as happy to see people and new things off his turf as well as on. He also needs to meet other dogs, in an appropriate setting (like training school). Students will tell me, "but he has Senior dog to play with, he's getting lots of dog socialization." Remember, Senior is part of the pack, and the puppy understands that. What your puppy needs to be comfortable with are dogs outside his pack.

Lack of proper socialization is the core reason for many behavioral problems. Can you overdo it? Never! Take him as many places as you can. Find appropriate play mates for him in the neighborhood. If you don't have children in the family, recruit neighbor children to come over and play properly with your puppy. If you are a single adult, make sure your puppy is interacting with folks of the opposite sex. More is better with socialization. It's much easier to tune down a dog who is overly exuberant and jumping on folks than to work with the shy dog who backs away in fear.

 W.O.W.: Training should start the moment you bring your pup home. This is the best time to get him started on the right paw!

Puppy Kindergarten at AllBreed

Jon and Riley "talking"

6
Speaking "Dog"

Let's get to the nitty gritty of understanding what our canine friends are telling us. Although it's already been said, it never hurts to repeat the fact that dogs do not do things out of spite, revenge or hate. These are human emotions. If your dog is chewing or defecating in the house, the message he's sending is not an emotional one. It's a flag that something has gone awry either physically or mentally with him, and that you need to respond to it immediately. Dogs tell us through physical acts what they are thinking. They never lie or pretend. When my Border collie smells a storm coming she becomes my black and white hemorrhoid. I don't need to turn on a weather report to tell me a storm is near. My dog has already done that.

I cringe at the words correction or punishment in connection with training a dog; or worse yet, slap, pinch or tap. Anyone who says it's not abusive to physically correct a dog with their hands or body should let someone slap them while they are trying to learn and see how much of the lesson they retain. Physical punishment doesn't train a dog, it only inhibits him from doing the behavior at the moment. If you want to teach a dog that hands do good things, then don't use them as negative tools by swatting or grabbing your dog.

The alpha roll, where we forcibly put dogs on their backs and sit over them staring at them, was the dominance exercise of choice for many trainers. Now think about this. How many dogs have you seen forcibly put another dog into a roll? I've seen many dogs on their own accord roll over for another dog. This is their version of saying "uncle" to the more dominant dog. If you force a dog or puppy into this position and he doesn't say "uncle," but instead fights back ,we then called this dog dominant. The owners were told they must continue with this exercise until the dog submitted. What we ended up doing was setting up folks to fail with their dogs. To do this exercise properly, students would need to time it right and accept nothing less than total, relaxed, submission. We inadvertently taught some of our dogs that having a person simply stand over you can be scary. Remember, dogs learn by association, so bending over could be misconstrued as the alpha roll in their minds.

I used this roll once, on an adult dog, and it was truly an instinctive move on my part because I certainly hadn't planned to. I was working with a dog who didn't want to walk on a leash. After a few minutes of inching him forward and praising him, he decided his only way out was to kill me. He jumped at my throat. I threw up my arm across my neck and watched as this dog chewed it up and down before he let go. When I didn't run away, he decided to make his point again, and came back at me. This time I caught him by either side of his face, threw him on his back on the ground and sat over him. I was holding his head between my two hands, leaning over him with my face very close to his telling him what I thought of him. It suddenly struck me that I had an aggressive, very scary dog under me - now what do I do? Luckily the dog was very still beneath me. The fact that I had responded to him quickly and in a fashion he understood sent a canine message to him that he had lost this one. I was lucky in that he did say "uncle." If he hadn't, I may not be here today. I firmly believe that if I had tried to strike him he would have taken up the challenge. Speaking "dog" probably saved my life in this incident. I later found out that owner of this dog corrected him with a belt. If indeed physical correction really worked, this dog should have been perfect. Instead he was a walking time bomb who thought the leash I put on him was a weapon.

There should be no place for violence in our lives, much less in training our dogs. If simply slapping or shaking your dog worked, I and other dog trainers would be out of business. Dogs do not hit each other, and rarely kill each other. Watch a mother with her pups and the most you'll see her do is give a little nip or growl, or pin a pup down softly with her mouth or paw to make a point. In my classes we have what is called "free play" at the end of the training session. Here the dogs are allowed to run and play with each other in a safe, supervised environment. This lets owners see how dogs interact with each other. I tell them to watch and learn as their dogs shoulder and push with their backsides while playfully growling and nipping at each other. The water bowl is always an interesting place as usually three or four dogs will decide to get a drink at once. There is an immediate understanding of who goes first, second and third.

Play is short, three to five minutes. Within that time the dogs have already decided who they like to play with most. It's interesting to see that dogs tend to gravitate towards other dogs with similar personalities and play styles. If they can assess each other so quickly and get so much said in a short time, why can't we? The answer is simple. We don't speak dog. We don't sniff each other, nor do we sniff our dogs to see what they're about. We use words to communicate and expect our dogs to understand everything we say. For example, on occasion I will ask my advanced students if they think their dogs understand and will obey the word down. Everyone always smiles and says "of course he does, we learned that weeks ago!" I go on to say, "great, let's test it!" The test is simple. The owner stands next to his dog and without moving a finger tells the dog to lay down. Usually two out of five dogs will respond correctly. The others will sit there and look at Mom or Dad and you can tell by their faces they must be thinking "so what's their problem today?" What the dog is waiting for is that hand, finger or body movement. Body language is what the dog pays attention to first, verbal second. My best experience with body language was with a wonderful student named Linda and her poodle, Oreo. Linda was having a hard time getting Oreo to wait on the recall command as he seemed to be anticipating and getting up before she called him. We did two tests with Linda and Oreo. First I had Linda stand very still, as she called him in. It took three tries before Linda was able to keep her own body still. Without knowing it she was moving her hands, then she moved her shoulders and lastly she moved her head. On all three occasions Oreo got up to come to her without her verbal command. When she finally held completely still and called Oreo, he just sat there and didn't move. I then had Linda bend slightly as she had been doing in class, but did not have her call verbally. Oreo was up and running as soon as she bent. He wasn't listening to what Mom said, he was watching for physical cues. What this means for Linda is that if Oreo was outside and far enough away that he couldn't see her physical cues, he may not respond as quickly to the verbal command. It would then be falsely assumed that Oreo was disobeying her on the recall when really he was just responding to how he had learned this command.

Hand signals are very easy to teach a dog. I think it would be interesting to run a class where no verbal cues were given, only physical ones. I'm willing to bet the dogs would learn quickly! Of course, it would be a very strange class for a human to be in! It's a great idea to teach both a hand signal and a verbal command, that way a dog will have no excuse for not complying!

Now that you know your dogs world is full of physical cues, you should do as much hands off training as possible. By this I mean don't be physically pushing or moving your dog into a sit next to you. Hands on can be distracting to him. Having you touch him is the ultimate in his book, and doing so will take his focus off his work and onto your touch. For example, it's a common mistake for students to physically lift up their dog if he's gone down on a sit/stay. I've watched a dog be picked up and placed into a sit, only to slink back into a down as soon as his owner gets across the ring. Let's put this into a human perspective. If, by accident, I found that, while watching TV with my husband, if I fell out of my chair he would come over, pick me up and rub my shoulders, I might make chair falling a nightly ritual. Goes to figure that if a dog finds out that every time he lays down, his owner comes over and touches him, that a smart dog would fall over a lot as this is pretty darn good in his book. Using our hands for praise and love is always acceptable. Your dog will find out soon enough that when he pleases you, hands are his reward!

Tone of Voice

When you're working with your dog, keep your tone quiet. Many trainers encourage students to yell NO when a dog does makes a mistake as simple as getting up from a stay. If you use a loud tone of voice for your every day training and communicating, then you have no where to go when your dog exhibits behaviors that are aggressive or dangerous to himself. If all his life he's heard you yelling, that one time it really does matter, he will tune you out. I train with a very quiet voice, and I insist my students do as well. I lower my tone slightly when I give a command, and I raise it up in tone when I praise. When I do raise my voice in volume, I have my dog's complete attention. I save my louder tones for when there is a scuffle amongst them, or one decides to challenge me, or someone is heading for the street. Take this thought into your dog training: loud is not firm and firm is not loud. You will never see the leader of a wolf pack barking out commands at the top of his voice. He is quiet, subtle and completely sure that everyone will do as he says.   The leader is confident, fair and completely sure of himself. He doesn't have to struggle for compliance, it's given freely. If we follow the example of the alpha wolf, we're sure to win with our dogs. So please, for the sake of your dog's ears as well as those around you, speak naturally to your dog. He'll appreciate and so will you!

Subtle Messages:

Dog language can be very subtle and can go unperceived by the untrained human. The act of simply walking away can send a huge message in the dog world. I did a behavioral consultation for a client whose dog was starting to act up a bit outside with the neighbors. He was becoming more protective and aggressive in his behavior when out in their own yard. We went through the usual questions, and when we came to how the grooming was going, she had an interesting answer. It seemed her dog didn't mind being brushed, but would only let her do it for a short time. He would slowly walk away from her, and rather than pursuing him, she decided he must have had enough and let him go. What he was telling her was "I'm in control and I'm tired of you." What she told him by letting him leave was "go ahead, you make the decision, you're the boss." Catching this communication between the two of them didn't drastically change his behavior, but it was a flag to a bigger part of the problem, which was the dog thinking he was in charge.

How often I've heard students say they had no clue what set off two dogs into a fight mode. One minute they were standing quietly and the next they attacked each other. It's not as invisible as we think, it's just that, as humans, we miss those little messages our dogs send each other. Learning to read your dog is an important lesson for all owners. Everything they are thinking can often be seen in the eyes or body of your dog. For example, I was teaching my advanced class a few months ago and one of my star students, Mako, was slipping a bit. He was moving on his stays and generally rebelling on just about everything Zig was asking of him. (Hey, we all have good days and bad, and this was not one of Mako's best.) Zig was doing an out of sight down stay with Mako. While he was out Mako got up, so I walked over, quietly took him by his collar and told him down. He ignored my command, so without a word I simply pulled down on his collar. I never reprimanded him, I simply didn't accept his behavior. As he went down he turned quickly to look at me, and the look clearly said, "I could bite you." Now Mako has had moments in his past where his behavior wasn't exactly stellar. I'll never forget how Mako's first night in beginner class went. As I went around to meet and introduce myself to dogs and handlers, Mako's response to me as I came up was to lunge at the end of his leash barking and growling. It took me six weeks before I could touch him in class, and six more before we trusted him with other people. We trained Mako with the clicker, an operant conditioning training tool. So back to the look. I immediately gave Mako my favorite phrases "I don't think so!" in a tone that means business (again, this is firm, not loud). His eyes softened, he dropped his head and he had that "oops, didn't mean it" look. Now if I had missed his message I may have set myself up for a bite. This would be because, in Mako's eyes, I ignored his first warning, and he might have felt he needed to take it further by escalating the behavior. Your dog will always be testing you, in small ways and sometimes larger ones. It's the small ones we often miss, which sends the wrong message to our dogs.

Misinterpreting Communication

Sometimes, without meaning to, we add to the problems by misinterpreting the communication our dogs are giving us. The story of Cooper and Jennifer is a classic tale. When I met Cooper, he was a 2 year old, very handsome, Golden Retriever who had been withdrawing from his human pack. Jennifer called me with the problem that Cooper wouldn't come in from their very large yard at night when she called him. It had become such a battle, that often she was leaving him outside all night because it was simply easier. We agreed on a consult date. When they arrived Cooper, who after giving me a very shallow, non-typical hello for a Golden, sniffed the room, then placed himself in a down as far away from us as he could get. It was odd to see a breed that is so people oriented act this way. As Jennifer and I began our consult, she told me that they had lost a boxer puppy about a year before. It was after the death of the puppy that Cooper began to show signs of depression and withdrawal. Jennifer took him to obedience class, thinking it would pull him out of his funk, and although he did well, she didn't see any spark in his eyes while he was working.

The problem was not that Cooper was still mourning the loss of a dog that had only spent a short time in his life, it came from the fact that he had lost his pack. Because Jennifer thought that being outside made Cooper happy, after the puppy died she started letting him out more and more on his own. His yard is large, and he could most certainly find things to keep him occupied. Jennifer thought, in her kindness, that this was the answer to replacing his loss. It did just the opposite. When the pack loses a member, there is a mourning, but it's a group participation. The pack doesn't split up and wander off alone. They always have each other. Cooper was detaching himself from the pack, but he was having help. He was beyond mourning for a lost puppy, he was mourning the loss of the pack relationship that our dogs thrive on. Not wanting to come in at night was a clear signal that he didn't feel an association with his human pack anymore.

Jennifer was told to go home and start keeping Cooper in the house, attached to her if necessary. She told me he would not like this, and would fuss to go out. The answer was easy, don't give in. If she did take him out he was to be exercised on leash, and if they were out in the yard and wanted him with, she was to have him on a long leash and keep him close. Recalls were practiced with his long leash on. "Check in" games were played. She would call Cooper, give him a treat and then walk away. He was being taught the word "come" didn't always means fun is over you have to come in. Inside the house he was allowed to hang with his human pack and re-orient himself with them.

After a month Jennifer called with excitement in her voice. Cooper was coming out of his shell. He was clearly happier with them, coming when called, and comfortable being in the house with them. It's been two years and Jennifer tells me that Cooper loves being with them more than ever. Jennifer knows she was part of Cooper's problem for not understanding the message being sent, but she was also very much part of his improvement!

Body Language

Body language is your dogs first and foremost form of communication. Because he comes into your house only knowing canine language, he may mistake some of our human traits as baffling and strange. Imagine if in your world the showing of teeth was a sign that someone was telling you to back off. Then you come into this new world where all the strange looking pack members show their teeth, and they seem to be pleased about it. Although at first surprising, you would quickly catch on to the fact that it seems to be a good thing, for this species. You also can't forget that it still is a warning sign with your own canine friends.

Your canine friend also shows you many physical signs of how they are feeling. Learning to read your own dog's body language is the first step to successful communication.   Dogs give us body signals trying to pacify or calm us. They will greet us with a lowered head, they will lick us, or lick their own lips. They will curl their body, either into you, or in front of you. They may urinate when you look at them or touch them. They may yawn, stretch, or casually scratch themselves. Remember, your dog has a very well honed form of communication among his own kind. Watching for the messages your dog is giving you will make you more aware of what your dog is feeling at the time. It can also be very frustrating for your dog, who jumps on you in greeting, because in his world that's a sign of play, excitement and friendship, and is told by his new pack member that this isn't acceptable. As a dog you would be in a quandary trying to find another way to show your excitement. What's a dog to do?

The Ignore Approach

Ignoring is a huge message your dog sends to you, or you can send to him. It tells the other pack member a couple things. It can say, "You're not important enough at this moment to pay attention to," or "You were inappropriate with me, so I'm leaving." The dog that takes two, three or more verbal commands on a simple exercise he knows well is telling you, "yada yada yada, I'll get to it when I'm good and ready. Can't you see I'm busy here?" I don't let a dog ignore me. I say a command only once, otherwise my dog will think that the command is a long sentence - "sit, sit, come on you know this command, sit." Being fair to my dog, I always say his name first so he knows I'm speaking to him. I get him to look at me before I continue with what I want him to do. If he's not looking at me, then he's not connected, and there's a good chance he'll ignore my command. Attention is important in communication. When your dog looks directly at you, the two of you are connected. Think about how you feel when you're talking to someone and they won't look at you because they're watching TV or lost in their own thoughts. I know from experience with my children that the phrases "look at me" or "pay attention" were often used. Somewhere along the line I figured out that children hear with their eyes, and whenever they started gazing in the opposite direction, their hearing would waiver! Dogs are the same.

You can also direct the ignore approach at your dog. If he's barking at you or pushing for attention, simply walking away clearly tells him you are not interested in him. Some dogs will then try the sneak attack by jumping on your legs as you walk away. Ignore this behavior as well, and in due time the dog is going to say "This doesn't work." Can we ignore all inappropriate behaviors? Of course not, but don't underestimate the power of ignoring.

Pain

Pain can quickly change the way your dog relates to you. Dogs that don't feel well can't say "gee Mom, I don't feel well today." Pain can manifest itself in unexpected acts of aggression by your dog. In the canine world, illness is a weakness. A weak dog is vulnerable, so the dog will try to hide his illness. As it gets worse, he will become more volatile in his reactions as a way to protect himself in his weakened state. As Dr. Hunter tells us, by the time a dog starts to show signs of pain or illness, it can be very severe. Dogs will live with minor aches and pains and not ever acknowledge it other than with inappropriate behavior. When I have a client call with a dog with behavioral problems, we always examine possible medical issues. I'll often send them off to their veterinarian for blood work to check thyroid levels or for x-rays on joints. A simple ear infection can set a dog on edge. Always be aware that if your dog's temperment starts to change, it isn't always that he's being naughty, it could be a medical problem.

WOW: Dogs speak clearly to us in many ways. Learning our dogs individual body messages can help both in training and the every day challenges. Changes in attitudes or personality should always be paid attention to. It may be a flag that your dog isn't feeling well.

7

Social skills

The three main areas dogs must master in order to live a long and harmonious life with their humans. are social, life saving and human pack skills.

SOCIAL SKILLS
- Able to interact with both humans and other dogs in a reasonable fashion
- Walk nicely on a soft leash
- Greet humans in acceptable manner
- Follow simple commands
- Be under calm control in public

PACK SKILLS
- Respect
- Trust
- Love

LIFE SAVING SKILLS
- Reliable Recall
- Down Stay
- Leave It
- Drop It
- Give

Canine Good Citizen graduates

Dogs will need their humans to train and guide them as they work towards acquiring these skills. These social etiquettes are based on human requirements.

JUMPING UP ON PEOPLE:

Remember in chapter two when we talked about hard wiring? Dogs come to us only knowing their canine world. For example, as I watched my parent's new Cairn Terrier, Reggie, interact with my nine year old border collie Jezzie, it was plain to see why he spent so much time jumping up on people as that is exactly how he tried to interact with Jezzie. From the moment he saw her he was in the air. He leapt at her face, jumped on her sides and bounced in front of her like a furry mexican jumping bean. When Jezzie lay down, he jumped into her face, except this time Jezzie said "stop" in dog language with small growl and a show of teeth. At first he was sure she was mistaken, after all, he was the cutest, most fun puppy in the world, didn't she know that? It took Jezzie two more times to make her point. Reggie finally said "oh, I get it," and walked away to play with his own toy. She never had to "knee" him, step on his toes or jerk him off with a leash, all of which we humans have tried on our dogs to handle such a problem. She was consistent with the fact that she didn't want him jumping, and every time he tried she simply said NO, in a firm, but very fair fashion. Although teeth were shown, she never used them. She did give him an alternate behavior by allowing him to sit or lay next to her. This seemed to satisfy him as I watched him happily chew his bone laying close to Jezzie. He never did try to entice her to play again, and he clearly understood what she would and would not tolerate.

It took Jezzie 15 minutes and a few reminders the rest of the week to teach this puppy that jumping on her was inappropriate. Why, then, does it take us so long to teach this?

First, let's look at what your dog is telling you when he jumps up:
- it's a form of greeting,
- it's a way to show excitement and happiness,
- it's a way to engage the other pack member into play mode,
- it's a way to get something away from another pack member,
- it's a way to get attention.

In looking at the reasons why a dog jumps, you can see there isn't a negative purpose in any of them. This means, when you think about it, that he's not being a bad dog, he's just being a dog. If we want him to communicate with us in a human fashion, we're going to have to teach him what's expected of him. It's amazing how fast they learn what works with dogs doesn't always work with humans.

Solving this canine puzzle means finding an alternate behavior that is appropriate for your dog. The solution should be easy, simply teach the dog to sit for attention. But training the dog to sit for you isn't enough. You must work with him to sit on command for other people as well (you'll see how this comes into play further on). The pot gets stirred more when we add the human element. Consistency is the key in training. In order to repeat a behavior over and over, a dog (as well as a human!) must be reminded. Think of how hard a habit was for you to break. For example, when I was about 14, I started using the word "bloody." It was the favorite word for the week. I would use it in sentences like "the bloody door wouldn't open." I refer to this as my "Ghost and Mrs. Muir" phase, as I had seen the movie and really liked the ghost. My parents didn't approve of this word, but my friends thought it was a great word and started using it themselves. Since I could use it one place, but not another, I would inevitably slip when around my parents and use the word. The ending to this story was that being a teenager meant it wouldn't be long and another word would become the "fave." My parents never did eliminate the word from my behavior, I was just smart enough not to use it around them.

In dog training, the same kind of sabotage can be going on. You work hard to give your dog an alternate behavior, and when you're around, it goes fairly well. I often hear, "he never jumps on me, just other people." That's a clear signal that a mixed message is being sent to the dog. It means you've done your job teaching what he can and cannot do with you, but you haven't transferred that to the rest of the world yet. You have to be there to teach him how to greet other people, he won't figure it out on his own. Other people, without meaning to, will encourage a jumping behavior. They get excited when they see your dog, they smile, use high tones, sometimes lift their hands up or bend over. They touch him, either by pushing him off or petting him. He gets exactly what he wants and he knows from experience that in this situation, this behavior always works. People pay attention to him, they can't help it. Remember, dogs will work for negative as well as positive responses. If jumping up on a person gets Mom to come over and pull him off, great, now he has two people paying attention to him! Teaching your dog to sit on command for someone else will help transfer the appropriate behavior to the outside world.

Here is the sequence in teaching the dog an alternate behavior to jumping:

1) **teach a solid sit**. Practice it everywhere, in the house, outside, in the park, at the pet store.

2) Have other people tell him to sit. Be there to enforce it if he opts to ignore the command. Use the "only one command" approach. In other words,

say it once, if the dog doesn't respond, guide him by using your finger tips or a gentle pull up on the collar. Don't let your helper repeat the command either. If a friend has to say "sit, sit, sit" while the dog is jumping, the dog will learn that with other folks you get to jump while they say the command!

3) Have him sit every time he gets attention, either from you or friends. Be sure the rest of the family is also following through with this exercise. This includes when he comes over to you while you're sitting on the couch and sticks his head under your arm for a pet. Tell him to sit first, then pet him. If he's crazy when you come home and you know he won't stop jumping, even with the sit command, ignore him for five minutes. Walk in and do a routine. By this I mean take off your coat, make your coffee, open your mail or change your clothes. End it by going to the doggie treat jar, turning to him and saying "sit." Give him the cookie, give him a quiet greeting, then take him outside. Repeat this routine for two weeks. It always amazes clients how quickly the dog figures out the new routine, and when they come home find a dog that races to sit and wait by the cookie jar rather than leaping on you.

4) Keep a leash handy when friends come over. Don't allow the wild behavior. Prepare him for company by leashing him and telling him to sit while they approach him. If he's really excited, then have your company ignore him until he settles down a bit. Some dogs take longer to relax when company comes over. Allow him as much time

as he needs so that he isn't set up to backfire into the old behavior of jumping and being silly.

5) If you're out on a walk in public and someone wants to pet your dog, make him sit first. This also allows him to get ready for the greeting, rather than being surprised. Dog bites can happen when people, either adults or children, come upon a dog quickly and the dog isn't prepared for the touch. I teach all my children in the kids classes that you must always, always ask before you pet a dog. Not every dog wants to be touched by you, no matter how cute the dog is. As the owner, you have the right to say no to someone who may want to pet your dog. The basset I co-own, Maybee, is a very shy girl. We have worked hard on this, and although she isn't a social butter-fly, she can handle herself well in a crowd, an obedience ring, or in my house. I do, however, have to prepare her when she meets new people. Because she's a basset, everyone assumes she is people friendly, and she can be in the right situation. If she is surprised though she will back up quickly. Preparing her makes the interaction better on both ends.

Overall, if you change the dogs approach to what gets them your attention, you'll be surprised how quickly they take on the new behavior.

BARKING - WHAT'S WITH ALL THAT NOISE?

Most cities have ordinances about barking dogs. They can vary from town to town, but here in White Bear the ordinance clearly states that a dog cannot bark for more than five minutes. I feel that is a very generous ordinance. Dogs bark for many reasons, but there is the key word, reason. If we ignore the barking, we're ignoring a message. A message that is ignored can manifest itself into another problem as the dog feels they have to take it to a higher level to be understood.

WHY?!!

Barking is just one way our dogs communicate with us and others, both human and animal. Our first job in managing this behavior is to understand why it's happening. Reasons are many for barking dogs, below are just a few!

1.   Fear. Dogs who are fearful will bark to scare away whatever it is they are afraid of. Dogs who bark at people walking by are always reinforced when they scare the person away. Of course, the person is simply walking by, but in the dog's mind, he's gotten rid of the scary thing! Next time he sees someone he will repeat the behavior, as it's very self-rewarding.

2.   Aggression. Dogs who are were not well socialized as puppies, or have a tendency for dog aggression in their breed, will bark at other dogs in a very different way than the fear barker. They will lunge and pull when on leash, and they will rush a fence.

3.   Boredom. Dogs that have nothing else to do (and remember the backyard is very boring after a while!) will bark to simply have something to do. For this barker you need to time how long he can be out before the barking begins and bring him in before he has a chance to start.

4.   Exercise. Dogs who aren't getting enough exercise will find their own way to burn off energy. Barking feels great and can tire them out! For this barker, you will notice that he barks every where at everything. Increasing his exercise, so he's tired (tongue hanging out, flopping on the floor!), will help decrease his need to bark. A mere walk around the neighborhood or park on a leash is not exercise for your dog (unless you have a basset hound!!!). Remember this motto, "A Tired Dog is a Good Dog!"

5.   Separation Anxiety. Being left alone can be a fearful thing for dogs who are extremely dependent on their pack. They bark in hopes of bringing you back to them.

There are many techniques to manage barking, depending on the cause. First, you will need to have a word (quiet, hush), and then you need to find a way to interrupt the behavior, because if you start to yell quiet while your dog is barking, he won't stop. As a matter of fact, he may really enjoy the fact that you've joined in!

Squirt Gun: This is a wonderful, nonpersonal tool that many owners find invaluable. It can be filled with water, or if your dog loves the squirt, put a small amount of vinegar in it to give the water a taste.

The squirt gun should be small so your dog doesn't really see it. Otherwise your dog will respect only the gun and not your command. When your dog is barking, tell him quiet, then follow it with a squirt of water. When he stops barking make him sit, and then praise him for following your command! Many folks carry a squirt gun with them on walks to interrupt inappropriate barking at other dogs or people.

Citronella Bark Collar: This is a very humane way to control the general nuisance barking. When the dog barks, a spray of citronella shoots out, spraying them under the chin. I like folks to try to be there when the barking starts and then say their quiet command as the dog begins to bark, thus he hears quiet and the citronella collar is spraying them. This puts power behind your word so the next time you say quiet and they don't have the collar on, they will listen.

Bringing the Dog In: Removing the dog from where he is barking and putting him in a time out in his kennel can be very effective. It simply teaches the dog that when you bark, and you ignore your quiet command, you're removed from the pack for a while.

BACKTALKING:
    Never allow a dog to back talk to you. In dog language, he's not saying very nice things to you if he standing in front of you demanding to get attention, food or anything else. If your dog does this, turn your back on him and walk away. No attention for that! If he follows you, then turn to him, tell him to sit and give him all the attention you want to!!!
    Always remember, a dog does what works (you'll see this in a lot of the management skills), so turn a bad behavior into a good one by giving your dog another way to express himself!

SOFT LEASH HEELING:
    Heeling is really a dance done by the two of you. To reach the desired finished product of a perfect heel you must both have the steps as well as the command down. Just like dancing, a simple push

one way or the other with your leash can turn your partner the wrong way (not that humans dance on leash, but we do direct our partners with a hand on the back!).

1.   Put your dog on your left side in a sit.
2.   Take your leash, put it over your right shoulder letting it come down your back and under your left arm.
3.   Put food in your left hand.
4.   Say the dog's name and the word heel.
5.   Step out with your left leg (that's a go leg!).
6.   Show the dog your food in your left hand. Put your left hand on your hip.
7.   Your dog should be walking with you on your left side, with his shoulder next to your knee.
8.   If he forges ahead, stop, while at the same time telling him wrong, heel. Bring him back into position.
9.   When you stop, immediately tell your dog to sit. Note: Your dog needs to be sitting in the direction you were walking and you are facing!!

TIPS ON HEELING

House Heeling: Start out with your dog on a leash walking through your house. Don't worry if it's a little tight as that will give your dog less chance to move out of position!

Back Yard Heeling: Take your dog out to your backyard on leash and work the heel exercise (if weather permits). If he can heel nicely there, then it's time for the next step.

Driveway Heeling: Take your dog to the driveway and heel up and down it. If you are getting a good response there, then it's time to hit the streets!!! Don't be in a rush to get your dog out on the street heeling. If he can't do it in the house, your backyard and the drive-way, there is very little chance he can handle it on the street. That will make this exercise a frustrating one for both of you!

Off-leash tips: When your dog follows you from room to room, encourage him to walk on your left side with you. Food in your hand, or just a small pet on the head will enforce to your dog that being on your left side is a fun place to be!!

KEEPING CONTROL

A dog that knows basic obedience is a much more welcome citizen in society than the dog that is lunging, pulling on his leash or barking. Consider basic obedience as your dog's key to social acceptance. When I take Jezzie, my companion dog, out with me into the public's eye, we receive many compliments on how well behaved she is. She is a pro at public relations work, I'll give her that, but what folks are seeing is a dog doing a solid down stay while I go about my business. She has been taught since she was a puppy that down/stay means just that, no matter where you are or what is going on. Society sees her as a well trained dog because she is under control. Of course she is well trained, but never underestimate the power of a solid down stay! A controlled dog is one that listens to basic commands when it counts. Be it a down stay, a sit or a reliable recall, it's all about having control of your dog's behavior.

INTERACTIONS WITH HUMANS AND DOGS

Dogs that are fearful of strangers or aggressive with other dogs have a harder time being socially accepted. Dogs exhibiting these characteristics are labeled with names like fear biter, shy dog, vicious or dominant. People often have the misconception that dogs will automatically like other dogs and will come preprogrammed on the appropriate behavior with them. Our job as humans is to help socialize our puppies at an early age so that they can interact easily with humans or canines. If you're working with an adult dog that missed out on this aspect of his growing up, you may want to solicit the help of a good behaviorist or dog trainer to begin a behavior modification plan for your dog.

Pack Skills

Pack skills are the glue in the relationship the two of you have. It's how you interact with each other on a day to day basis. Trust, respect and love are all things that the human/canine bond thrives on. Like any skill, these must be practiced and honed. When we can give as well as receive these three pieces, we have the basis for a harmonious relationship with dog.

TRUST:

In order to obey you, he must trust you. This means he knows that you will never hit him, scream at him, or hurt him. For some dogs, this will take longer than others because of their past. But please remember, not every dog that comes from the shelter was abused. He may be soft, and thus shows an overabundance of submission, but this is not fear. Do not unintentionally enforce behaviors you don't want. For example, if your dog is showing a fear of something, do not pet him, telling him it's ok. In his mind you are praising him for his behavior, and next time he'll be even more afraid because you told him it was the right way to be. A fearful dog must trust that if it doesn't bother you, it's cool. Instead of coddling him, get him busy doing something for you, or start playing an obedience game. He will learn trust by watching you!

RESPECT:

Respect comes from understanding where his place is in the pack. This goes back to the dominance issues that are so important. If he feels he's above you on the chain of life, he'll let you know by only following your commands when he feels like it, or growling at you if you try to take something he feels is his. A dog shows respect by wanting to please us (although this comes in varying degrees depending on breed). He listens to what he's told and doesn't growl, snap or bite at us or our human friends. People will often make the mistake of thinking that because they are the humans they are the bosses, and the boss is always shown respect. Your canine friend looks at you as a pack member, and he respects rank, not species. There are never any equals in a dog pack. Everyone has a place in the rank, and no one shares a place.

LOVE:

Love is the easiest for humans to show to their dogs. What we have to be sure of is that we don't love our dogs so much that we lose the respect and trust that is so important in our relationship. Love means you may have to do something to your dog that you know is good for him, but hard for you. For some that is saying the word NO. To others it may be containing them. No matter what, love will most certainly be an important ingredient in obtaining a harmonious relationship with your dog. There is nothing more wonderful than looking into a pair of soft brown eyes that say "I Love You" so very clearly!

As you work on your relationship with your dog, keep in mind a few hard facts. One is that dogs DO NOT have human emotions, in that they don't do things out of revenge, hate or spite. They do have a strong sense of loyalty. That would come from being pack animals. Dogs are not human, but in order to understand their behaviors we have put human emotions to their actions. Once you understand that your dog does things because he is a canine, you may find it easier to understand why he chews your underwear or urinates on your bed!

There is nothing more wonderful than the relationship between a human and a dog when things are in order. Nothing can compare with the gentle, quiet companionship that dogs give us. But in order to get that we must do our part by taking the time to train our dog, understand his behaviors and respond to his needs. The dog/human bond is one that has withstood the sands of time. Dogs have adapted to our ever changing lifestyles as best they can. How different a dog's life is from even just 40 years ago! They are truly amazing animals in their capability to adapt. We are lucky to have such animals at our side, sharing our lives.

Life Saving Skills

These are skills we need to teach our dogs that may very well save their lives some day. This category includes a reliable recall, down stay, leave it, drop it and give commands, and also proper car etiquette.

THE RELIABLE RECALL

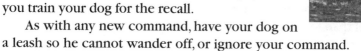

This is the most important command your
dog needs to learn. It could possibly save his life,
and of course, keep him home. This is where
your name game and connection word pay off as
you train your dog for the recall.

As with any new command, have your dog on
a leash so he cannot wander off, or ignore your command.

1.   With your dog on a leash, let him wander out in front of you.
2.   Say his name
3.   When he's looking at you (and remember, if a dog isn't looking at
you when you give a command, there is a good chance he will ignore
you!), give the command COME.
4.   If need be, give a gentle pull on the leash. Typically if you've
done your name game homework, he will turn and start toward you
without any help.
5.   As soon as he's coming toward you, CONNECT! Use your special
word, i.e., Yes, Good, etc.
6.   Reach down and take his collar (this teaches him he must have
his collar touched before he gets his reward).
7.   Give high value treats when first teaching this exercise, then
lower the value and begin random treating.
8.   If your dog doesn't come to you, go to him, repeat the command
and move backwards. Dogs love to play chase, so engage him in that
game while he's learning come.

CASUAL TRAINING TIPS FOR THE RELIABLE RECALL:

Call him from the back door, give him a treat and then send him
back into the yard. This teaches your dog that you don't only call
him from outside to go in and will help with the dog that just stands
in the yard and looks at you while you call him from the door.

Play puppy in the middle in the house, perhaps between the
kitchen and living room with each person calling him and treating
him when he gets there. The come word will take on a whole new
meaning!

Practice everywhere you can. In the house, outside, call them while walking on leash in the neighborhood. If taking your dog out into an area where he can be off leash, keep a long lead (30-40 feet) on him and play "check in." This is where you will reward him for coming up to you on his own. It teaches him that being close to you is very good for him! Also call him to you on command, treat him and send him on his way. Too often folks call their dogs only to end the play, and a smart dog says this word come isn't so great! Don't forget to use your connection word as soon as he's coming towards you. This is your "invisible leash."

RULES OF RECALL:
Never call your dog with the recall word if you need to do something uncomfortable. The word Come should only be used for good things. If you need to get your dog for something other than praise, then go get them, don't call them.

CAR ETIQUETTE

So often as I'm driving, I see dogs hanging their heads out of car windows, or bouncing back and forth from front to back seat. To enjoy traveling with your dog, car etiquette must be taught. Dogs loose in the car without proper restraint or training are putting themselves and their owners in danger. Think about having a dog loose in the back seat behind you. One quick stop and he will fly forward, possibly through the front window or hitting your head from behind. Either scenario isn't very pretty. Although dogs love to hang their heads out car windows, it puts them in danger of getting things in their eyes or nose. Dogs sitting in the laps of drivers can be crushed from their owners or hit by the air bag. Dogs have also been known to jump out of open car windows, putting themselves and oncoming traffic at risk. I once found a dog running down a highway. I stopped and called to him, and he immediately came over. He had a collar with a tag on it, so off we went to the nearest gas station and I made a call. The woman who answered said her husband and son had taken the dog to the store with them. She had no idea the dog was loose, which meant the guys were still inside shopping and probably didn't know he was gone. We assumed he jumped out of the open truck window, as it was summer and warm out. This story had a happy ending, but not all do.

When purchasing a dog, people seldom think about their vehicles in comparison to the size of the dog they are buying. Owning a small car and getting a large dog can cause some unexpected logistical problems. The safest and most comfortable way for your dog to travel would be in a plastic or wire crate that is secured to the floor. Being in a crate means your dog can sleep while you drive. If you were to get into an accident, he wouldn't be tossed around the car. Another option is a doggie seat belt. These belts latch onto your existing belt, and the dog is able to sit and ride. This means he can look out the window and still be secure if the car were to make a quick stop. If either of these are not an option, then the floor is the next best place for your dog. Having him on the floor means that if you do stop quickly, he will have less space to travel in.

Teaching your dog to be quiet while you travel could take some time. I tell my students to simply practice riding in the car by putting the dog in, starting the car and going nowhere. Enforce your down stay if the dog is loose. He needs to learn that he has to listen to this command even when he's in this moving crate! If he's a whiner, bring along an interrupter and train him not to cry. For yourself bring along a cup of coffee or a pop, and settle in for 20-30 minutes as you work your dog in the car. During the first 10-15 times your dog is practicing in the car, give him a good treat to chew on. This will make the thought of going in the car fun and exciting. It doesn't take dogs long to learn that going in the car means something good is going to happen, either you're going to the park or visiting friends.

Dogs that are fearful of the car should be introduced slowly, using the technique above, simply sitting in the car. With some dogs we've had to work for weeks just to get them to go in and out comfortably. Making special treats available only when they're in the car can help move along this process. Take your time, and never loose your temper or try to physically correct this fearful dog.

Using the "wait" command is also important. Teach your dog that he cannot leave the car until you say OK. This will give you control as you open the door and eliminates the possibility of your dog rushing out before you can leash him or make sure the environment is safe for him. Practice opening the door and insisting your dog stay. Once you see him relax, give him the OK and let him get out.

We should always be thinking safety for our dogs, just as we do for ourselves.

DROP IT, LEAVE IT, AND GIVE:

These commands can warn your dog of a potentially dangerous item or situation. As hard as we try, there is always that one time that the dog saw something we didn't and either tried to eat it or pick it up. My basset Gus came out into the living room one day with a knife in his mouth. He was bringing it to show me, which is a game we have taught him. I tried to be as calm as possible, and in a controlled voice told him to drop it. He did. Teaching drop it isn't always enough though, as often the dog will want to pick it up again. I told Gus to leave it after he dropped the knife, so he walked away with a "gee, what a party pooper" kind of look. Where did he get the knife? He found it on the floor where it must have dropped earlier in the day. Had I planned for that? Of course not, but because my dog understands the drop it command I can safely say we avoided what could have been a nasty accident.

The difference between drop it and give is that give means put it in my hand. Drop it means let it go out of your mouth now. I use my give command when playing fetch, as I'm rather a lazy owner who doesn't want to bend over all the time to get the ball!

WOW: A well balanced dog is one that is reasonably proficient in all three areas. When a dog is strongly lacking in any or all of the three, the inbalance can cause problems with the overall relationship between the owner and the dog.

8

How to say NO

There is a lot of controversy on using the word no. Some say you should never use it, others say you should. My feeling is the word NO should be the opposite of your connection word. No is simply a marker word that lets the dog understand that the behavior he is doing is not acceptable and that a consequence will follow. When teaching any behavior you must not just say No. You must also say, No, but you CAN do this. So often I hear folks say "all I say is NO to this puppy!" My response is "What do you say after that?" For example, if a puppy jumps on you, say NO, then say sit. We must give our dogs alternate behaviors - for every non-acceptable behavior, we should give them an acceptable one.

TEACHING NO!

No, like any other command, needs to be taught. Just yelling it at the dog and thinking they understand is not very realistic. If you haven't taught the dog that when you say No, there is a consequence to be dealt with, your dog will ignore the word because it means nothing to him. Your tone can be scary to them, but not the word. Again, with every NO should come an alternative behavior command from you so that you can then praise the dog and end on a good note. If your dog doesn't do the alternate behavior, then the consequence of NO may be going to his crate or being ignored.

A consequence should TRAIN your dog, not SHAME your dog! If we're truly training our dogs, then using the words "correction" or "punishment" shouldn't be in our vocabularies. What we want to do

is interrupt the behavior. In other words, using a squirt gun, time out, ignoring them - those are all very fair and understandable interrupters. I've seen puppies that, when squirted with a gun act like "that didn"t hurt," yet they did not repeat the behavior. Don't look for a puppy to roll into a submissive posture or lower his head or run and hide after a consequence. It should simply interrupt the behavior or be a little uncomfortable, but you should still be able to go on and give them the positive thing they should have done instead. Remember, any training tool used for interrupting (like the squirt gun) should ALWAYS be hidden behind your back...surprise! It should NEVER be used as a threat. Then the negative is actually the article, and not your NO word. We want the word to have the power, not the training tool. Students often tell me that all they have to do is pick up the squirt gun and the dog stops barking. What is the dog respecting? Certainly not the word. If this student were to say No, quiet, without the squirt gun in her hand, the dog would ignore her. The formula should be: Wrong behavior (i.e. barking) = verbal No Bark command followed by interrupter, followed by Alternate Behavior = Good Dog!

The time should fit the crime: in other words, be fair about your consequence. If a simple "ah ah" can stop a behavior, then use it. If the puppy is in full play bite mode, then a time out may be more appropriate.

SO WHAT IS A FAIR INTERRUPTER?

Squirt guns, with water, or if your pup says he loves it, put a little vinegar in with the water to make it taste bad. The squirt gun should be very small, so it can hide in your hand. Down commands can also be used as interrupters. I was once training a border collie to stay within it's yard. The owners had already taught the dog to lie down every time she saw a car. It made border training a bit tricky, but I was so very impressed with the owner's ingenuity in coming up with their own way to interrupt this dogs chase drive and channel it towards something not only safe, but positive. Needless to say though, it made our training go a bit slower as they lived on a busy street!

Motion sensors can be great interrupters. Set them up by the trash can or the counter that your dog loves to cruise. You can teach the dog that this sound is like a verbal NO from you. When you hear the sensor go off, follow through with your consequence. This teaches the dog that you have eyes even when you're not in the room!

Time out: using the crate for a consequence is certainly ok as long as you are using it for good things as well. As a child I was often sent to my room. I loved my room, and after my mother told me how much trouble I was in, she would say those wonderful words "go to your room!" Once I got in my room she would leave me alone. I was able to read my books, lay in my bed, or sleep. Did I mind it? I never minded the place, but I did mind the fact that I was being forced to stay there. When I've decided my dog is in need of a time out I will take him by his collar, walk him to the crate, mumbling all the way about his behavior. Once he is in the crate, everything stops. I don't stand out there and berate him for being bad, I simply walk away. A smart dog will be happy to be in his safe place rather than out with the old grump. Time outs should be short, 5-10 minutes. It's just giving your dog a little time to think about what just happened.

As mentioned in chapter 6, you can send a huge message to your dog by ignoring him. Sometimes behaviors are done simply to get your attention, and if you just shrug your shoulders and walk away, the dog is told, that didn't work. So for example, if your dog barks at you for attention, try turning and walking away from him. This can also work for item stealers, who take things of yours just to get you to come and get it. If it isn't dangerous for the dog, your lack of response will make this game very boring! Conversely, if your dog is taking a while to respond to your commands, his message to you is that he's running the game and he'll get to you when he feels like it. Don't let him do this! Remember, say his name, connect, give the command - one time only!

Face Talks: I've often taken my dog's face in my hands, and gotten very close and personal to have a talk with her. I make solid eye contact and I tell her what's what in my world. I'll use this if my dog has blatantly opted to ignore what I'm telling them to do. This is just a simple reminder that I'm boss, and you need to listen. I only use face talks with my own dogs, never dogs that I don't have a solid pack relationship with.

With any of the consequences, the most important thing to remember is to be consistent. Don't bluff your dog, always follow through. If he gets away with something once, he'll try it again. Getting the word No taught to your dog can save his life. At my house, No is the ultimate bad word. It means stop what you're doing now and wait for further instruction from me!

With more than one dog in the house, it's a good idea to have a separate "no" word for each dog. In my house, No is the universal, "everybody is in trouble" word. If I were to say No to one, they would all feel the affect of the negativity. By giving each dog their own negative word, I can single out that dog, give him/her his negative word, and the other dogs are not affected. Gus, the youngest of the group has the word "pain" (which came from a phrase used often with him!). When I say "pain," Gus moves quickly out, knowing full well he's in trouble. The others wonder what's up with Gus, but aren't worried. These words were used and taught just like the No, command. I really like the fact that I can single out a dog and the others are unaffected.

WOW: Overall, remember that saying No is part of the learning process for your dog. You must be able to tell him when he's doing something wrong, and have him understand what he just did. A good NO command can save your dog's life, and tag the behavior you don't want quickly and fairly.

Flint "being cute"

9

Are they really bad?

Clients call me with every complaint known to the canine/human world. I have a philosophy about dogs with problems. Stick with me as I continue, because there is a method to this madness!

I spent 20 years of my life working in the corporate world. There were always problems, as is usual when you have a diverse group of people working together. Problems were typically the result of human oversight, lack of training, or not enough time or manpower to do the job. The best way I found to handle a problem was two-fold. One, stop fussing and complaining about it. Instead, focus on the solution. It's amazing what happens when you do that. Suddenly the problem wasn't as upsetting as it had been because I was taking the time and energy I put into complaining and was channeling it into a solution. Taking ownership of a problem instead of pushing it off as "his or her problem, not mine" made it easier to solve. You can't change other people, but in changing yourself or how you approach something can affect others in a positive way. I never knew a problem that when handled correctly didn't end up with someone finding a better way to do the job. Without problems we wouldn't grow and become better at what we do. It forces us to analyze the formula and think "outside the box."

So how does this corporate story fit in with dog training and behavior problems? To start with, dogs who misbehave (who are not medically impaired) are simply acting on behaviors that worked in the past. There are three ways we encourage bad behavior. We ignore it, encourage it or respond emotionally.

For instance, to blame a dog for jumping up on company and labeling him as "out of control" does not solve the problem. When clients come to me we sit down and talk. Many questions are asked. Often as we're chatting, you can see the light come on in their eyes as they begin to realize that they own some of their dog's problems or behavior.

I tell them this story. Imagine that you recently started a new job. You were trained on how to do this job the day you started. You are now very comfortable with it, and feel you're doing great. Then one day you come into work and your boss asks you to come into his office. He isn't smiling. He proceeds to tell you that you're doing the whole job wrong and that you either need to get with the program or leave. Now, he doesn't tell you what is expected, or how to accomplish this.   Without training you can only rely on what worked in the past. You'll go back to your desk, frustrated.   If you try to figure it out on your own, chances are you'll be wrong, and the boss will let you go.   I've seen lots of dogs at the shelter surrendered because they couldn't do the job right.

Use this same scenario with your dog that started jumping on you as a puppy, and it was cute. Now he's bigger, and it's inappropriate as well as dangerous. To be fair to the dog, before the owner decides he's out of control, he should be a good boss, and have an alternate behavior for him to do that will still get the job done, but keep them all happy. Otherwise the dog will continue to do what worked before, and perhaps escalating it to a higher level if he thinks it's necessary.

Once we see what we're doing to encourage a behavior we can then begin to problem solve and convince the dog there is a better way.

It's also good to remember that many of the inappropriate behaviors we see are breed specific and/or driven. Dogs that were bred to work all day on the farm, or hunt for us in the field, will demonstrate these behaviors in actions that can drive a human to extremes.

When you think about it, dogs have had most of what they've been bred to do outsourced by human technology or social advancement. We no longer needs dogs to kill rats or herd sheep at the level they used to. The number of "working dogs" is becoming fewer and fewer, while the number of family dogs increases. This means that when you take a dog into your home that was bred to do something, he is going to follow his breed instinct.

If any of you have ever lost a job because you were layed off or outsourced, remember what you did. Your first instinct was to find a job that was like your old one. After all, that's where your skills and knowledge lay. You likely found a job that was similar, where you could use some of the skills. Otherwise you would start over in a new job, where perhaps you aren't doing the exactly the same work, but were able to fall back on the skills learned previously. In the dog world we call this channeling. For instance, if you have ever owned a beagle, you saw from day one that his nose is never off the ground. Now you have no need for this skill, but it's a driving instinct in this beagle to use his nose. Your job is to find alternate ways for him to use this "skill" of his so that he doesn't come up with his own, usually inappropriate ways, of using it. Teaching him find it games that can be played with the children in the house on a rainy day, can make for one happy, busy beagle. The sport of tracking is very satisfying for a hound whose nose never sleeps!

It's important for dog owners to know how to take their dog's natural traits and find alternate channels for them. Giving your dog an outlet for his inbred drive will make everyone happy.

Separation Anxiety

This is a syndrome that has caught the publics eye. It has become a catch all for many unwanted behaviors. True separation anxiety needs to be diagnosed by not only your veterinarian, but a behaviorist as well. Some of the symptoms of separation anxiety could be attributed to medical problems. A behaviorist will have a number of managing or modifying exercises that may relieve the dog of his stress.

Medications are now available to help dogs with this. Unfortunately I've seen it misused a number of times. People make the mistake of thinking that by simply giving their dog a pill the bad behavior will go away. Medication should be the last resort to rehabilitating a dog. When it has been deemed appropriate for use, it should always be under the supervision of your veterinarian and your behaviorist. As stated above, medication alone will not modify the behavior, training must also be included .

In the world we live in , it's not surprising that many of our dogs are anxious. Dogs are often left alone for eight to ten hours a day. As humans we suffer from "doggie guilt." When we come home we shower our dogs with attention. Because we've been gone all day we allow the dog to follow us everywhere (I've heard of clients that even have to let their dogs come into the bathroom with them or the dog whines and scratches at the door). These clients typically don't use the crate or any other form of separation while they are home because after all, the dog has been alone all day. What we can create is a dog that says being alone is always bad. The only time life is good is when I'm with my owner. This form of bonding is not a healthy one, and can drive a canine to display some very undesirable behaviors.

So what are the symptoms of Separation Anxiety? Anxiety shows itself in many forms. A dog may whine, bark or howl before, during, or after you leave. They may keep up the noise for hours after they've been left alone. They may chew destructively, either on items or furniture. They may mutilate themselves by chewing on feet or pulling out hair. Anxious dogs will defecate or urinate in the house as a result of the stress of being alone.

When you are home, anxious dogs never let you out of their sight. They follow you from room to room, in a seemingly obsessive way. They whine at the window as you go out for your mail. They greet you with exaggerated exuberance, even if you've only been gone for one minute.

Anxiety in dogs is a time consuming disorder. It creates stress not only in the dog, but the owner as well. The owner, as stated above, always feels guilty about the way their dog acts. I usually hear statements like, "he's mad at me when I leave so he defecates in the house," or "after I left for work he decided to get revenge so he ripped up all the pillows." Remember, dogs don't do things out of revenge or spite or because they're mad. Separation anxiety is a fancy word for an over abundance of stress. Dogs handle stress in many ways, all of which are usually inappropriate. Chewing, defecating and barking are stress busters for them. The hardest thing for some people to realize is that the dog isn't doing this as a personal vandeta. He's responding physically to the situation, in the only way he can. Emotion has nothing to do with it.

In all potential anxiety cases, there are some steps to be taken before it can be properly diagnosed.

1) Put a tape recorder on to run for an hour while you're out. True separation anxiety will continue beyond the one hour tape.

2) Whenever your dog displays a nervous behavior over a period of time (a month or so) a check with the vet is in order. Anytime there is a change in your dog's behavior you want to be sure it isn't due to a medical reason.

3) If the dog comes back clear from the vet, talking to a behaviorist is your next step. Remember, we own part of our dog's behavior, so a good behaviorist will be giving you exercises to help relieve the dogs stress when being left alone.

4) If the behaviorist diagnoses the dog as having separation anxiety, then a behavioral modification plan and perhaps drug therapy will be developed for your dog. Your behaviorist should work with your veterinarian on this.

In summary, separation anxiety should not be taken lightly. Dogs do not outgrow these symptoms without human intervention. Sometimes it's as simple as changing the routine in the morning. Most often it's more complicated, but usually treatable. Again, it takes time and energy on our parts. Remember that behavior modification can take months of work before we see progress.

Stress

Stress alone can play a large part in our dogs behavior. You may be thinking, "Now what does that dog have to worry about? He's fed every day and has a roof over his head."   Dogs react to their environment. A simple thing like moving to a new house can put stress on a dog. Dogs enjoy routine. Change, for some, can be unsettling (sound like humans? You bet!). During behavior consults one of the first questions I'll ask is if there have been any changes in the household lately. Has someone moved out or in. Did someone get a new job and the hours changed? Have there been any relation-ship problems (I don't counsel for these!). Dogs are very in tune with our feelings and without meaning to we can send our own negative thoughts right into our dogs. I once had a client who was distraught over a certain situation. Her dog started to have what seemed to be allergies, scratching all the time and biting at himself. She called me because he was also chewing up articles in the house, which he hadn't done before. As we talked she shared her situation with me, and we then could clearly see that the dog was reacting to the way she was feeling. I know from my own experiences in dealing with a negative person how it affected me. It got so I didn't even want to talk to her anymore because I would walk away from our interaction feeling badly.

Dogs pay attention to everything in their environment, and they respond to it. Living with teenagers means frequent disputes over house rules, etc., at my house. Every time we get into these sometimes heated discussions, my dogs all disappear from the room. They're not comfortable with the stress we're creating. I can imagine that if we lived that way every day our dogs would have to respond to it somehow. Just as with separation anxiety, dogs will chew, bark, defecate or hide. Does this mean you can never have an argument with your spouse or child in front of your dog? Of course not, but it's important that you know that dogs react to their environment in physical ways. Some can handle more stress than others. What's most important is that before you call your dog naughty, think about what's going on in his environment and see if there is a correlation between his behavior and the overall atmosphere at home.

Garbage Lovers

Ah, the garbage can. That wonderful, delectable container that holds everything a dog could want and more! What dog could resist? Not many, to be sure. Even my own dog, Jezzie, who is about as perfect as a dog could be decided lately that she could no longer hold herself back. Jezzie was the dog who earned her privelege of being loose in the house when she was less than a year old. I could leave food on the floor and this dog wouldn't touch it. Since she turned nine, she has begun to show some behaviors that I would have expected out of a much younger dog. We came home one day to find the entire kitchen covered in garbage. It had been neatly spread out, like a human would set up a buffet. I immediately thought the bassets had gotten out. I went into the dog room, and there were the bassets, sleeping away in their kennels, doors still locked. I went upstairs and there was Ms. Jezzie with ketchup on her chin. Busted big time! Afterwards we wondered if perhaps she had been doing it all along, but was smart enough to do it only when the other dogs were loose. I'm sure not, but it was certainly an entertaining thought!

So how can you stop a dog from going into the garbage? There is a thought out there that if you don't feed them people food that they won't go into the garbage. That doesn't work for me as I've seen my dogs eating things outside that I know I have never given them, be it dead frogs, worms, or the most delectable, goose droppings.

Think about how your dog sees the garbage can; as food you don't want. It's obvious to them you don't want it because you've left it unguarded! Remember the wolf pack, and how the alpha pair always eats first, then the rest come in. Once you leave the house, you've in essence told the dog, "I don't want that anymore, go for it!" We humans have tried every trick in the book to outsmart these canines. The first is to put a lid on the can. I had one that could only be opened by stepping on the little lever on the floor. My old lab, Tucker, figured that one out in a few weeks. The bassets are amazing

at how, with their short legs, they can topple a can. I guess if you put sixty pounds against anything, it's bound to give!

My clients will tell me, "but he know's he's done wrong, as soon as I come into the house he slinks away!" Sorry, but he doesn't think that way. As he's munching away on a left over potato, he's only thinking about how good it was that you left this for him. He knows he can't go into it when you're home, after all that would be rude. You still have rights to it by your presence. But, once you're gone, all bets are off. He does know, however, that garbage on the floor + you coming in door = trouble. You've taught him to respond that way, because every time you see garbage and him together you respond negatively. So being the smart dog he is, he knows how to act when all the pieces come together. As he's eating the garbage, you're not there, so the puzzle isn't complete, the human element hasn't entered yet.

So now that you know it's a natural dog act to get into garbage, how can you stop it? My best advice is to put the garbage away. We always put it up on the counter (remember, we're working with short legged bassets here, it's hard to knock off a can from the counter). If you have a more agile or larger dog, you may have to put the garbage can under the sink (although I've heard of folks that have had to put baby locks on cabinets because the dogs were able to open them up!) or out in the garage as you leave. Confining your dog may be your best answer, either in a crate or an area. Remember that being loose is a privilege, and if you can't trust them they should be confined. So if your dog gets into the garbage, it's your fault. Michael and I just look at each other when we come home to it, and say "I thought you put the garbage can up!" We always blame each other, never the dog!

A final thought; if your dog does get into the garbage, be sure to talk to your vet about things he may have eaten. Your vet may give you instructions on how to make the dog vomit. He may want you to watch the dog for any ill effects, or he may want to see him. Dogs will eat anything, including plastic wrappers, wire or tin foil, to name just a few. These things may not pass well through his system, and he may start to vomit, with diarrhea or signs of pain. If he shows any of these, a trip to the doctor should be immediate as x-rays will need to be taken to see what the cause is.

Counter Cruising

Just like garbage cans, this can be a tough one to work with. My bassets are the worst offenders. It amazes me how they can get enough height to get bags of bread or cookies off the counter. I was working up in my office one day and heard a loud thud,

followed by three others. I crept quietly downstairs to find my basset Kelsey jumping at the counter. With each jump she was getting a bit higher, trying to get at a bag of bread she smelled, because she certainly couldn't see it! She had decided to use the springboard approach. She was concentrating so hard on her task that she didn't hear me, so when I said "Hey, what are you doing?' she, needless to say, jumped higher than ever! Too bad I was there, as she would have made it with that one.

Dogs are also very good at figuring out ways to get up there. Gus, my youngest basset will use a chair every time to get up and see what's on the table. He's totally blatant about it, as he will do it when I'm in the living room watching tv. I can see him out there, so it's not like he can get away with it. Time out in the crate is always my interrupter, but I guess he figures it's worth it, as I know he will repeat this behavior with every chance he gets.

Kelsey proved to me that she could reason out things to get at what she wanted. Years ago I taught community education dog obedience classes. They were held in the city garage (oh, those were the days!). Graduation night always includes cookies, doggie treats and pop. I brought the treats in a large cooler, and had set them up on the workbench. I left the cooler next to it. Kelsey was allowed to walk free, as she was a well trained dog, right? Well, as I'm running my class through graduation, someone said "Look, Kelsey is helping herself!" She had jumped up on the cooler, and then put her front feet on the bench, and was munching happily on the cookies (she had opted for the cookies over doggie treats!). Had I thought she could do that? No, I hadn't, silly me. We all laughed about it, and Kelsey was never invited to another graduation!

So how can we stop counter cruising? You'll hear all kinds of ideas, including putting cans up there so they topple down and make a noise, or putting your cookie pans on the edge. There is the sand paper approach, or cutting strips of those plastic floor runners that have little nubbins on them, and place them on the counter. The bottom line is that dogs will do just about anything to get at food. They may not take the bread when the interrupter is on the counter, but they will continue to try. I always ask folks, where were you when this happened? And why is the dog allowed in the kitchen if he misbehaves in there? At our house, no one can walk into the kitchen unless I'm in there.   If I catch a dog going into the kitchen, I call them out. If I'm having a big problem, I will block off the doorway. Putting a small jingle bell on your dog will also help you know where they are and alert you to the fact they're in the kitchen. By the way, my dogs never counter cruise when I'm in the room. That's the human element we've talked about before. They are well aware of the fact that I "guard" these things, and they can't attempt to take them when I'm there. When I'm not, they think it's fair game!

Some problems we can only manage, not fix. Garbage cans and counter cruising are two of those. You can be as creative as you want, but in the long run, the dog will probably go back to his original behavior. The reward is so great that he can overcome the fear of retribution.

Stealing items

So you have a thief for a dog. He loves to grab your underwear or your pens or anything that seems to be of value or have your scent. You chase him around the house, trying to get it back. He laughs at you and really seems to enjoy it. Well, he does enjoy it. Watch two dogs play as one takes a toy and the other chases after him, trying to get it. I've watched my dogs play "swap em," where one dog wants what the other has, so he goes and gets a toy, entices the other dog who drops what he has, and the two swap. Your dog feels that if it's yours, it would be fun to take it to entice you into a game.

The way to handle this is two fold. One, keep a leash on your dog so that if he does take something, you can simply take hold of the leash, say "give," and walk away. No reaction either negative or positive, which means no reward for the dog. With my springer mix, Flint, who puts everything in his mouth, we took a different approach. I praised him for picking up something, saying what a good boy he was, and then asked him "what do you have?" Instead of walking to him, I let him come over to me (sitting on the floor is usually a position your dog cannot resist you in!). When he came over I would say "give" (see how important this command is to teach before they start giving you trouble?), and praise him for doing so. Flint now brings me things just to show me. I've been given dimes, gloves and tissues (without one rip in them) to name just a few. I took a behavior that could have been very obnoxious with this dog and turned it into an acceptable one, taking his natural instinct and channeling it. This method of training can backfire on you though. I decided to teach my basset Gus to fetch by rewarding him for bringing me toys. Now, whenever I'm eating a snack out in the living room, Gus brings me toys and drops them at my feet, giving me a look that says, "look what I brought you, feed me quick!' I have had up to eight toys brought to me during the course of eating one apple. The good news is I can ignore this behavior because I haven't asked him to do anything. But I will tell you that his drive to bring me things is very strong, and that will be a huge plus when we step into the obedience ring for dumbbell work.

Treasure guarding

Treasures to your dog can be food, treats, toys, or even something as silly as a candy wrapper. The problem arises when the dog feels he must keep these treasures at all costs. Aggressive behavior is usually the course of action taken by the dog. The food bowl is a common battleground. Depending on how far the dog has taken to guarding will dictate how we approach it. If we have a dog that starts growling as soon as someone walks by his food bowl as he's eating, I have the client fill up his or her pockets with the best treats they can find, for instance, roast beef. As they walk by the dog, they drop a large piece of beef and continue on. A minute later they walk by again, once more dropping a large piece of beef. The client is told to do this without bending, stooping or stopping. As the dog picks up the food, I tell the client to praise the dog as they leave the immediate area. This may go on for a week or more. Soon the dog will look forward to having the owner walk by, as something good will be coming. Eventually we will have the owner bend as he drops the food, and over course of time, will eventually put the food into the dog's bowl. The final outcome will be that the owner can take the food bowl, put in a goodie, and return the bowl to the dog better than when he took it.

Treasures are not always something we anticipate. For instance, if you give your dog a pigs ear, and he's never had one, he may respond in a very unsettling manner as he runs off to hide in a corner to eat this exciting and very special treat. When clients tell me that their dogs get aggressive over pigs ears or rawhide bones, my response is, don't give it to them anymore. Sounds too simple to work, but there are some things that dogs consider precious beyond reason. Be it a treat, a toy or a bed - whatever it is that causes the unwanted behavior should be tossed, never to be seen again!

The Human Element

Behaviors can be driven by the human element as well. In the following lists of unwanted behaviors, see how often we create the issue for the dog.

SHYNESS:
The shy dog can be a hard nut to crack. Typically they start out

as puppies with very little confidence. They cower, won't approach anything they perceive as scary. They shake or bark and because they are fearful, they may also bite. When trying to figure out what's going on, we need to look a number of things. Breeding can play a part in shyness as it can be inherited. Lack of proper socializiation can also play a large role. Sometimes it can be breed specific, as certain dogs can have a tendency towards shyness.

As humans, our hearts melt when we see a dog shiver and shake. Our first instinct is to make it all better by soothing it and speaking softly. As we stroke them we're telling them by our touch that they should be afraid. Remember, touch is reinforcement. You use petting when you're happy with your dog. You would never pet your dog if he had just tipped over your garbage can. So from the dog's point of view, he feels his fear is a good thing, and if you continue to reward your dog for this, he will eventually escalate it, because if a little fear seems to please you, more would be better! We have to remember that these are canines not human. You should not react to a canine in the same manner you would a human.

Dogs look at us as their leaders, so in the shy dogs case the first step is to build up the confidence of your four footed friend. Start by simply not acknowledging the fear in any way except to say, "hey, look at that, isn't it cool?" Well, ok, you don't have so say those exact words, but you certainly get my drift here. Being confident yourself around the scary thing, be it a person or lawn mower, is something your dog can read. Remember he pays attention to your body language and the tone of your voice. It's also good to give the dog something else to do.

Let's imagine a scenario of a dog who's afraid of people. Our dog is afraid of any stranger even looking at him. He dives behind his owners legs, peering out carefully. If the stranger continues towards him he runs to the end of his leash. If the stranger doesn't stop his approach, this fearful dog may feel like he has no other recourse but to attack, since flight has been eliminated. In the meantime the owner is telling the dog to "be nice." We often find that owners set up their dogs to react in a certain way. In this case the owner had seen this behavior over and over, so as soon as the stranger came to pet his dog, the owner tensed up, probably as the stranger was approaching. The dog feels the tension coming from his owner (remember, dogs read our body language all the time). The dog sees the stranger and thinks "gee, Mom is afraid of this man, I should be too." This can also manifest itself into the dog who lunges out and tries to attack or bite strangers while on leash with his owner. If our dog is reading something negative from his owner, please remember that he doesn't have a clue that the owner is tense because of him. He's sure it's the stranger causing the tension.

To help this fearful dog work through this problem, the owner needs to do some homework first. The connection word can help a lot here, as the owner could then connect when the dog displays appropriate behavior. Teaching a reliable sit would also be required before you hit the streets working on this. Also pay attention to your dogs space requirements. How close can a person get before he goes into his fear mode? Paying close attention to body language will help you read your dog so that you can make proactive decisions on what he should be doing. Trying to get a dog already in flight mode to sit may be very difficult, if not impossible.

So you're ready. Your dog knows that when you say "yes," he's on the right track. He also understands the word "wrong". He will sit for you on the first command, and you know that he starts to get uncomfortable with strangers when they're about 15 feet away. Arming yourself with high value treats, it's time to go to the walking path in your area. Find a place 30 feet away from the path. Somewhere where your dog can see people, but is well outside his range of fear. Work for five minutes only, having your dog by your side. As soon as you see a person put your dog into sit, connect with him and feed him. As he sits there, seeing the person, your job is to be a cheerleader, telling him "yes" and treat for as long as he's demonstrating good behavior. Because you've started far out of his fear range, this should be a pretty easy task to accomplish. If he acts up in any way, quietly tell him "wrong," put him back into his sit and connect. Be very generous with your food for the right behavior. If he's reacting fearfully, back him further away to start with. Be sure you're backing him up after he's done a good sit and settled, and not while he's barking in fear mode. A smart dog could misread that and think "gee, in order to get away from the bad person all I have to do is bark and Mom backs up!" After five minutes leave. Come back to the same place the next day and repeat the exercise, but move a few feet closer to the path. Every time you see a person coming, get happy, tell your dog to sit and feed him. Again, stay for a short duration. Leave on a good note not a bad one. On each session you should be moving closer and closer to the path. If you find that your dog is not ready to move closer, then take him back to where he was comfortable the day before and keep working.

Now you're wondering, ok, how does this help my dog accept strangers? What we're doing with the exercise above is teaching the dog that every time he sees someone, his owner is happy, and he is fed. After a month of doing this, a smart dog is going to tie it all together, understanding that people mean food, and that just seeing them seems to make the world a happy place.

Once you're able to sit by the path with people walking by and your dog is happily eating his treats and ignoring them, it's time for the next step. Depending on the level of fear your dog has with strangers will dictate how you handle the next level of training. With this step, I would ask friends to help, and I would work off the dog's turf (in other words, not in the house or his yard). Meet your friend at the park (preferably the same place you've been training him). Tell him to bring a treat to share with your dog. Start out by having your friend amiably approach the two of you, ignoring the dog, with the treat in his pocket. Greet each other, then start connecting with your dog as he shows the good behavior. Tell your dog to sit, but not stay. Have your friend keep ignoring the dog. When your friend is about four feet away from the two of you, have him stop and drop a few pieces of treats around his feet. If your dog is still comfortable, then you approach your friend. Here is where good acting skills come into play. As you stop to chat with your friend, you're very happy and calm (this is why we ask friends to help out!). Let the dog choose to come forward. As you're chatting, your dog will most likely find the food at your friend's feet. As he finds it, connect with him and praise him. If he sniffs your friend's leg or hand, connect again, and have your friend drop another piece of that great treat he brought.

Typically this is where we want to stop the exercise. End it by shaking hands or patting each other, smiling and leaving. Notice we didn't have the friend try to touch the dog. Moving too fast is a common mistake people make when dealing with behavior problems. Puppy steps are the best way, small but progressive. Behavior problems usually take months of work to modify. People are always hoping for a quick cure, but there isn't one. A dog that has been showing a certain behavior for months or years, will take more than just a few weeks to turn it around.

Back to our shy dog. You can see the path we're taking here is to make every interaction this dog has with a stranger a good one. Pieces are added when the dog is ready to handle more. When will your dog be ready? Don't worry, they'll tell you. When you think your dog is ready to be touched by your friend, remember to always let the dog approach the person first. If the dog seems to be very comfortably standing near the person, perhaps sniffing them, looking for food, then it's time to use that sit again. Have your friend tell the dog to sit. When the dog does, have your friend connect, and give a treat. Still no touch, just food. But now the dog is responding to a stranger's command, and getting rewarded for it. Once your dog is sitting calmly for your friend, then it's time to add the touch. Give your friend a larger than usual treat to give the dog after he's told the dog to sit. As your dog is busy chewing this nice hunk of roast beef have your friend calmy take his hand, which is already by the dog, and gently stroke a shoulder. As he's stroking the owner should be connecting with "yes!" Your friend need only stroke him once or twice, then stop. Exercise over, you'll go for more at a later date. Always keep your dog wanting more, that way when the opportunity comes up to earn goodies he's excited to come back to it!

As you can see, working a shy dog is a slow process. I know because of my own experience with Maybee, who is now nearly five years old. In her case we tried everything out there. I made the ultimate mistake of thinking she would outgrow it. She didn't, it just got worse. At a year and a half she was so fearful that when someone approached her she would back up, lower herself and growl. I had a big wake up call when during a training class she snapped at the instructor who tried to do a simple exam on the stand exercise. I was mortified. I started using any method I could think of to extinguish this behavior. I first had everyone feed her. I didn't do this in the way explained above, I did it the way the trainers told me. Have people come up and feed her. Well, every time someone came up, she would back up and lower herself and sometimes even growl. The person with the food would say soothing words, crouch down and hold out their hand with the food. She would creep forward, snatch the food and come back to me. Guess what I taught her with that one. Show the fearful behavior and get fed! So that didn't work. I went on to correcting her, first with a squirt gun and later with a collar. Neither did the trick. She then saw people as things that were bad for her. Finally my breeder suggested I use the clicker. The clicker is an operant condition sound that we put with food. Sound familiar? You're right, the connection word is the same idea. I began using the clicker and Maybee and I pioneered the above approach to working with a shy dog. Before long she was jumping up on people to get the click and food from them. She is still not a social butterfly, and will, on occasion, do what I refer to as a back fire, reverting back to the old behavior for a moment. Remember, habits die hard with us as well as our dogs. I've since changed her click to a word. She earned her breed championship along with her first obedience title, Companion Dog, and we're stepping into the obedience ring again soon to obtain her second obedience title, Companion Dog Excellent. She also excels in agility and tracking, and we will be giving those titles a chase as well. When I look at Maybee I see a dog who, with the wrong owners, could have been a candidate for euthanasia. She would have taken her fear way beyond what was socially acceptable. Her fear, as stated before, was not because of lack of socialization, it was something she came hard wired with. Simply getting this dog out and about wasn't going to change her. End of story with Maybee is that she taught me invaluable lessons on how to to handle the shy dog. She is a good example of taking a problem and finding a solution for the betterment of both of us!

THE AGGRESSIVE DOG:

I could write a whole book on aggression. There are many causes, which take time and energy to uncover. We often never find the cause, we simply have to take the behavior and work with it. Know that dogs who seem to be protective of us when we're not asking for it are really protecting themselves. Clients tell me that Fluffy won't let strangers approach them when they're out on a walk. Depending on what is going on with the relationship between the owner and dog, a couple of things could be coming into play to enforce this behavior. 1) If the dog doesn't have a clear understanding that you the owner are the leader and that he doesn't have to worry about things, he may feel he has to defend his pack because he knows you won't. 2) In accordance with pack rules, he may also think of you as a possession. Sorry, but I don't like having a dog think of me as a bone to protect from others. 3) He is fearful and instead of flight he's decided he needs to fight.

Aggression should never be allowed to continue. I always give owners kudos for calling me after the first aggressive incident rather than waiting to see if it happens again. Let me give you a small lesson on aggression. If the dog felt justified in his behavior, he will, given time, and without behavior modification, repeat it. One of the worst things we do for our dogs is give them excuses. I've heard many, including, he was sleeping and didn't know what he did, or he only does it now and then, or the best one is, "he's a good dog except he bites." In my book, as in many others, if he bites he is not a good dog. He's a scary dog that can't be trusted. It always amazes me how people will live in abusive relationships with their dogs, where it's the owners being abused. I've seen bruises, bites, and scars from dogs who are still living with their owners and continuing their aggressive behavior. Bottom line, if your dog has shown any aggression, be it over food, space, toys, or attention, or any thing else, do not wait to see what happens. An aggressive dog is a walking law suit. You could loose your house, your possessions, not to mention your dog.

Working on modifying aggressive tendencies in a dog should be done under a professional's eye. Because aggression has so many twists and turns, I cannot write tried and true methods; each case is different and requires an individual approach. I will say this though, that any trainer who guarantees that they can change your dog is a trainer to avoid. These are living, breathing beings we are working with. They are not machines. I expect a guarantee from my mechanic for my car repairs. Dogs are not cars, they have personalities, and most importantly, they have memories. These memories can get in the way of managing or modifying a behavior. I would also avoid trainers who use harsh methods. Remember, violence begets violence. If we're working with an aggressive dog, beating or hanging him into submission is not treating the problem, we're simply reacting to the behavior. With any behavior problem we need to know what triggers the dog. It's most important to be proactive rather than reactive when working with an aggressive dog.

INAPPROPRIATE HUMAN RESPONSES:

As I stated earlier, we tend to encourage behaviors by our own responses to the dog. For instance, many dogs are afraid of thunder and when it storms they begin to shake or cower. Well meaning owners will try to hold their dogs through a storm, or sit by them petting them and telling them it's ok. Remember what petting tells the dog? This dog is understanding clearly that storms are scary, because you've told them so.

Sometime dogs will work for negative responses as well. A true story is one of Reggie, my parent's puppy. He's a Cairn Terrier, very full of himself as terriers tend to be. He is having some trouble housebreaking, and at the age of 5 months is still urinating in the house. He tends to do it mostly when Dad leaves and shuts a door behind him. Reggie, although he loves my mother, doesn't like to be left behind. While Dad is out, he will urinate right in the path of where Dad is returning. Dad finds the spot, says "what's that?" and proceeds to verbally correct Reggie. I saw this happen when I took care of him for two weeks while they were out of town. It happened while I was in the bathroom. I could actually hear the urine hitting the floor right outside the bathroom door. Sure enough, I opened the door and there is Reggie, standing back a ways looking at me like, "see what I did? What are you going to do?" Well, I did what Dad did, I said "no, bad dog, what did you do?" Do you know what Reggie did? He ran around the house at top speed, happy as could be about the fact that I was giving him attention. He didn't cower, he didn't run away in fear, he was getting attention and he didn't care how. I finally figured out his game by accident. I was on the phone working. I had been on the phone for about 30 minutes and Reggie had been sleeping by my feet. The door to the outside was six feet away, and he is good about going to it and waiting. I watched him get up, move away about 8 feet, look straight at me and urinate. Now I'm on the phone, so nothing could be said. I turned away from him and he stopped. He came over and looked at me as if to say, "hey, what's up, aren't you mad?" When I finished the phone call I grabbed the cleaning cloth and spray. I didn't say a word to Reggie, as a matter of fact, I ignored him. While I was scrubbing the carpet he came over and watched, then decided to try to grab the cloth, because that might get a reaction. I pushed him off once, then put him in his kennel, never saying a word. It became clear that Reggie does this for attention, so the new approach to Reggie's housebreaking is to ignore the mistakes. Would this work for every dog? Of course not, but remember I told you in the introduction that dogs tell us clearly what works and what doesn't. For Reggie, having even the negative attention of being verbally corrected was fun for him, and urinating in the house made it work. I have never ignored a dog for a housebreaking mistake before. That just means I had never had a dog who needed this approach. Remember that dogs love attention, and sometimes by yelling or chasing we're actually buying into what they wanted, our attention!

If you're finding that your corrections aren't working, sit back and think for a moment what the dog may be getting out of this. I once knew a Great Dane, who had an owner who did the alpha roll with her as a pup. When this dog grew up, the owner would still use the alpha roll as a correction for aggression (mostly growling). It seemed the aggression was getting worse and the owner was alpha rolling at least a couple of times a week. I took the dog for a week for training. At one point during training she growled at me, so I did what the owner had been doing as I had suspected she had her own agenda for doing this. As soon as I alpha rolled her she began to play. She loved the fact that she and I were wrestling around. It then became clear that she was demonstrating these behaviors because in her mind it was a prerequisite for play.   Needless to say the alpha roll was history. We began doing down stays instead and the aggressive behavior lessened with her owner.

Hormones

If you have chosen to keep your dog intact, in other words, not have them spayed or neutered, you must understand the power of hormones. An intact male dog is always looking at other dogs as possible competition for procreation. Procreation is always on the mind of an unaltered male. He thinks it, eats it, breathes it. He can smell a female in heat up to five miles away if the wind is right. He may be inappropriate with other members of the house that he feels are less than he is. This can show up as growling at a child who tries to take something from him, or snapping at a family member for trying to make him do something he didn't want to do. Statistics show that unaltered male dogs are more apt to bite or get into dog fights than neutered males.

Unaltered females are not always a treat to live with either. Having one in my home for four and a half years was plenty for me. They have mood swings. They don't always play well with other females. Maybee went into four false pregnancies during her four years, each one worse than the other. She walked around for two months sure she was pregnant. She gained weight, she filled up with milk, she ate more, and she was cranky! Then one day she must have thought she had delivered. She came over to me while I was sitting in a chair and gently dropped a stuffed toy into my lap. I thought she wanted to play, so I tossed the toy which landed close to my since past on sweetie, Dara. She ran over, went after Dara in a very hostile action, grabbed her toy and ran off. She layed down with this toy next to her. Obviously this was her "baby" and silly me had tossed it away! We just had her spayed a few months ago, and life has taken a change for the better. She's easier going, not as combative with the other dogs, and sweeter to me.

My rule of thumb for my students is, if you're purchasing a pet, then alter it. We have enough unwanted puppies in our humane societies, and as I said before, breeding should only be done to better the breed, not to make money or do it for the experience. In our case, because we co-owned Maybee we were under contract to have one litter if she was championed. She did earn her breed championship, so we were bound by our contract to breed her. The breeder chose the sire, and helped us throughout the entire process with her expertise.

Hormones can make for some ugly behaviors, so be a responsible pet owner and alter them at the appropriate age. If you decide to wait, remember that these instinctual behaviors that are happening now can eventually be learned behaviors, which are harder to turn around. Talk to your vet about the right time to alter your dog. It's also healthier for your pet to be altered as it reduces the risk of cancer in both males and females.

The word and memory response

Without us knowing, expecially if you've adopted a dog that has a history with another owner, words can trigger an unwanted response. For example, if you have a dog you recently adopted from the shelter, you may find that saying the word NO makes the dog quiver and shake. Does this mean you can never say no to this dog? People often mistakenly think they can't correct their dog because it scares them. You must, of course, be able to correct the dog when he's made a mistake, so this would be an instance where changing the word would help. The next time the dog makes a mistake, use the word "purple," (any word will do, this is simply an example) and follow through with a down stay, a time out, or whatever fits the crime. The dog will then learn that "purple" means he did wrong, but it doesn't trigger the memory response that NO did.

Do the same thing when you have trouble with the word come.

If, somewhere along the line, the dog learned a really rotten version of come, such that whenever he hears it he runs the other way hoping Mom will chase him, it's time to change the word. Take a new word like "here," and retrain the recall from the beginning. To the dog, come meant chase game, and his memory response was to run and play. The new word will take on the memory response of always coming when called, as it was trained the right way.

So before you think your dog is being naughty, either aggressively or playfully, take the time to think what this word may mean to him. In our human mind, we're sure we've made our intention clear to the dog, and that he is just plain ignoring what we want. In the dog's mind, he has a different version of what that word means. Always trust the dog to tell the truth. He doesn't lie or cheat. Verbal noises (and that is what our commands are the the dog) take on various meanings, and it's when the human and dog have different interpretations of the "noise" that trouble ensues.

W.O.W. Never underestimate the role you play in your dogs behavior. They come to us with clean slates, and it's what we write on it that helps shape and mold their behaviors. Some we can change, some we can't, but we can manage. Dogs are amazing animals in the way they adapt to our human way of life.

10
Student stories

I wanted to have a chapter where a few of my students could share their stories about life with their dogs. I told them it could be about anything they wanted. The following are a few wonderful stories, followed by my usual W.O.W.!

Dottie's Story
Kerry Teel, loving owner of Dottie, 3 year old Dalmation

I remember when I first saw the beady, little brown eyes and pointy nose peering over the glass in the puppy room at the Humane Society. She was only 3 months old at the time and had already been a part of a family who didn't want her. It was inevitable, I laid eyes on the spotted puppy, and left with a new best friend. Yep, Dottie picked me out of every visitor that came to see her. I had already done my homework and knew what was needed and expected for us to live a long and happy life together.

Training was of the utmost importance...not just housebreaking. It would be important for her to know the basics, and more. Dottie would need work, because she was wary of strangers. Her biggest fear, however, was men with beards. Deb worked with her through her board and train program and she emerged a different dog and just kept getting better from there. Dottie and I worked our way through various other classes with Deb, until the little Dalmatian fearful of most everyone got her Canine Good Citizen title last spring.

Dottie is the reason I'm now involved with Dalmatian Rescue. It is incredible how many Dalmatians (let alone other breeds popularized by movies & commercials) are in need of rescue just like Dottie. Dogs of all ages wanting to find a family, the right family, to love them.

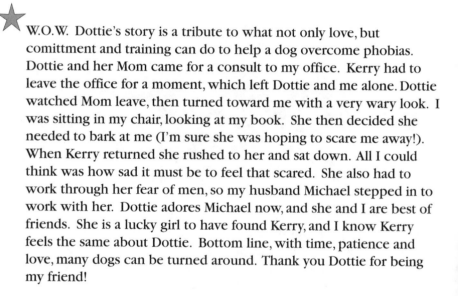

W.O.W. Dottie's story is a tribute to what not only love, but comittment and training can do to help a dog overcome phobias. Dottie and her Mom came for a consult to my office. Kerry had to leave the office for a moment, which left Dottie and me alone. Dottie watched Mom leave, then turned toward me with a very wary look. I was sitting in my chair, looking at my book. She then decided she needed to bark at me (I'm sure she was hoping to scare me away!). When Kerry returned she rushed to her and sat down. All I could think was how sad it must be to feel that scared. She also had to work through her fear of men, so my husband Michael stepped in to work with her. Dottie adores Michael now, and she and I are best of friends. She is a lucky girl to have found Kerry, and I know Kerry feels the same about Dottie. Bottom line, with time, patience and love, many dogs can be turned around. Thank you Dottie for being my friend!

Riley's Story - Give and Take

Jon and Kerrie Nelson, loving owners of Riley, a 1-1/2 yr old Basset Hound

Our basset hound, Riley, is possessive. When he was 3 months old, I went to take some paper out of his mouth and he growled. Unfortunately, I didn't correct his behavior right away because it had startled me, and the lesson had already been learned. Riley realized that we wouldn't try to take things from him if he growled. Deb suggested we play the give game. Whenever he had something (good or bad), we would say the word "give" and then show him we had a treat. When he dropped the object, or let me take it out of his mouth, he would get the treat and lots of praise. This seemed to be working; the only exception was if he had something he considered a "special" treat, like a pig's ear. If we spoke to him or walked nearby while he was chewing on this, he would growl, get up and go to another room. I didn't want to encourage this behavior by ignoring it, and finally figured out that it was in the way I approached him. The last time I gave him one, I walked up to him and matter-of-factly opened his mouth and took it. Even though I was a little apprehensive, I did not let my body language or voice show it, which caught him off guard. He then got a ton of praise and his favorite snack. He has drastically improved over the last year and we no longer have to bribe him if we need to take something out of his mouth.

W.O.W. Dogs know by our body language if we're telling the truth or not. Our words may say one thing, but when our body says another our dogs don't miss it. Kerrie and Jon are first time dog owners, so this was all new to them. Riley will take advantage of every inch he's given, and if he thinks there is so much as a hint of uncertainty he will take it. Always be confident, both verbally and physically with your dog, remember, they're watching you!

Button's and Duke's Story - "Busted!"
Cyndi Rohl, loving owner of Buttons and Duke, Miniature Schnauzers

On a quiet Saturday afternoon in July I decided to relax with Dillinger and Al Capone in the solitude of my bedroom. This being one of the most interesting books I have read in a long time. The room was peaceful and very quiet with bright sunlight gliding across the multicolor comforter and then sliding on to the thick warm carpet.

My comfortable recliner is placed in the south corner of the bedroom off to one side. This must be the perfect crime scene for our two miniature schnauzers, Buttons and Duke (AKA gray dog and black dog). The solitude of the house must've been what provoked the boredom in the dogs. As I looked up over my rose colored bifocals the two cohorts walked slowly and skillfully, like it has happened before, into the room from the partly opened French doors.

As the two trouble makers edged around the half closed door and in past the wicker basket, Duke, the black dog, chewed on Button's, the gray dog's ears. As they rolled around on the floor, not noticing me in the recliner, being as quiet as possible, the two hounds moved on to their point of crime, the large ceramic wastepaper basket under the sink in the bay area of the bedroom.

The white tile is very slippery for the two artful hounds and just as they danced to the great grand slam to dump the wastebasket I yelled out a plaintiff "BUSTED" and at that the two little rascals looked at me for a heartbeat and ran off at top speed with gray dog in the lead! Black dog took the corner at 100 mph and they both

covered the stairway in two gigantic leaps. I followed the two wonder dogs only to find one dog under the table and one under the
chair.

This is a problem when we go out or the house is empty for a
period of time. I come to our bedroom only to find the basket and
it's contents everywhere. Why do they do this? And why just that
bathroom and not one of the other bathrooms?

W.O.W. Dogs love to hang out where our scent is the heaviest. This
is the bathroom that Cyndi uses the most. Tissues with our scent are
in the basket, and dogs that are feeling a bit stressed by the owner
being gone or out of sight will often seek out the strongest scent.
That is why our underwear and socks are such treasures for our dogs.
They have our heavy scent. I guess we could find it a compliment
that our dogs love us so much they always want our scent around!

Thea's Story - No Jump Training

Erica Pye, loving owner of Thea, a 1 yr old Golden Retriever

My golden retriever puppy was notorious for charging at me and jumping all over me to get me to pet her.

To get her to stop jumping on me, I trained her that when I was standing the only way I would pet her was if she was in the down position. When she approached me and started to jump, I would say "No jump! Down!" and put my hands behind my back so that she knew I wouldn't pet her. Sometimes I would even have to turn my back on her. Once she was down I would praise and pet her. If she got up, I would immediately stop petting her until she went back down on her own. She quickly learned what I wanted and now when she charges towards me she drops into a fabulous down, right at my feet! No more jumping!

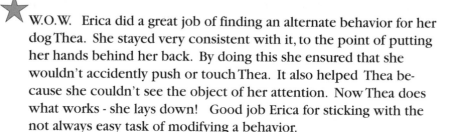

W.O.W. Erica did a great job of finding an alternate behavior for her dog Thea. She stayed very consistent with it, to the point of putting her hands behind her back. By doing this she ensured that she wouldn't accidently push or touch Thea. It also helped Thea because she couldn't see the object of her attention. Now Thea does what works - she lays down!   Good job Erica for sticking with the not always easy task of modifying a behavior.

No More chewing
Erica Pye and her three dogs

My three dogs have a large collection of every kind of chew toy you can imagine, yet I would frequently find them, surrounded by their own toys, chewing on my throw pillows, rugs or magazines. One day I found a basket that I decided to use as a toy box. I gathered up all their toys and placed them in the basket. Suddenly, all the toys became interesting again. The dogs enthusiastically dug through the basket to see what was in it, as if they had never seen the toys before. Now every night I put all their toys in the basket and the dogs wake up to "brand new" toys each morning. I haven't lost a throw pillow since!

W.O.W.   Dogs always love things that don't belong to them. They are notorious thieves and are typically pleased with themselves when they find something of ours to play with. Keeping a toy box in the living room is a great idea. Another idea would be to only keep in five toys (out of the 20 plus you probably have!) and circulate them. I change our dog's toy box every week, or I sneak a new toy or chew bones into the box. They are always checking it out, and when the "old" toys have been gone for a while they suddenly become new!

Olivia and her friend, Nixon

11
Kids and dogs

There are no two ways around it, kids and dogs love each other. The problem arises when the two try to play with each other on their own terms. How many times have you seen a child dress up the puppy or hug and squeeze them to show love and affection. In retrospect, I can't tell you how many stories I've heard of puppies and dogs that treat the children as littermates, chasing them, biting at their clothes and stealing their toys.

The good news is there is a middle road for these two very different, yet similar species to co-exist. It takes adult supervision and training, both for the child and the dog, but it can certainly be obtained.

Respect between canine and child

No matter how old the child is, it's important to teach them to respect a dog. By this I mean show them the dogs teeth and tell them that any dog, no matter how nice, can bite. Teach them to leave a dog alone when he's eating or chewing a bone. Don't let them play in the dogs crate, that's his house and not theirs.

Petting a dog in the right way is important, as children tend to move quickly, putting their hands down by the top of the head and then pulling them back. They often hold their hands above their heads, which encourages a dog to jump on them. Tell them to keep their hands low. Teach your child to pet the dog on his shoulder or chest. Tell him to keep his face away from the dogs mouth. Many children bend down, wanting to kiss the dog on the muzzle, which can be a formula for a bite, as a playful dog will see it as an invitation to play (think about the dogs you've seen playing together, who are always putting their mouths on each others face). A fearful dog may find this human is way too close for comfort and react by biting, and a dominant dog may decide to tell this child to "back off" with a growl, snap or actual bite.

I'm always surprised how many adults don't know that they, as well as their children, should always ask before they pet a strange dog. I once did a demo with Jezebelle for a group of about 40 cub scouts and their parents. We were there early, and as everyone was coming in, many of the families came over to see the dog. When we began our demo my first question to the group was "how many of you met Jezebelle?" A number of hands went up. I then asked "how many of you asked me if you could pet Jezzie before you met her?" At this point only a few hands went up, mostly children. The adults were the worst of the group, coming over and casually putting their hands on Jezzie. You could see the light come on over the adult's heads as they realized that they too could have been bitten. Someone in the group then asked me, "has she ever bitten anyone?" My response was "not yet, but she's capable of it." As a responsible owner I know that given the right situation she could react as a canine. Never think that a dog won't bite. As parents, if we don't educate our children how will they know? Unfortunately many children are bitten for that very reason. They didn't ask, they came up on a dog suddenly and they put their face down to say hello.

You can best teach this to your child by coming up behind him one day and startling him. Then let him know that his dog will react the same way if he doesn't properly announce himself, and that dogs will often use their teeth when they are startled.

Also teach your child the right way to feed the dog. Children should be taught to make a plate out of their hands, putting the food in the middle, and offering it to the dog. This does a couple of things. It eliminates the chance of little fingers getting nipped. It also reduces the chance of the child pulling back the food before the dog has gotten it, which would prompt the dog to jump on the child. They should offer it with their hands low, as the dog wouldn't see it if the child held his hand up too high. Once the dog has taken the food off the child's hand, tell them to go wash their plate!

Involvement with the training:

Any child three or over should be involved with the training of the dog. By this I mean they should be watching the adults train the dog. In a controlled environment, one where there is few distractions for the dog, the child can give it simple commands. With an adult to help, the child can learn a fair and productive way to interact with the dog. Children really enjoy being able to tell their dogs what to do. If the child isn't shown the proper way to work with the dog, they can end up getting bitten or being afraid of the dog.

Be sure you're helping the dog listen to the child. If the dog ignores the child's command, you will be there to guide the dog into position. The child can then praise the dog and try it again. When my son Jake was three years old he was walking my basset hound Kelsey on a leash through the neighborhood. I was always there with him, but Kelsey, who was two when she was able to do this safely with him, enjoyed herself immensely and the two became best friends.

Fun games for kids and dogs to play

Folks always ask me, if the children shouldn't run and rough house with the dog, what else can they do together? My answer is, plenty. Games are the stuff life is made of for both kids and dogs. Here are few I think your children will enjoy playing with your dog:

Hide and Seek: Nothing better than a good game of hide and seek when it's raining out. If the dog has good recall, or is responding well to his name, this game can go on for as long as your child's creative mind keeps finding places to hide! One person will need to hold the dog (or if the dog knows the stay command, the child can put the dog in a down stay, leave the room and then call him from his hiding place). Have the child call the dog. When the dog finds the child, have him give the dog a treat, a kiss, and start again! Dogs are very good at finding children hiding in closets or under beds.

Find It: This game is a little different than hide and seek because you will be hiding a treat for the dog to find. Teach the dog to sniff the food you have in your hand. Tell him to stay, or have someone hold him. Put the food down in the middle of the room where he can see it. Go back to the dog and tell him to "find it!" Of course he will run out and get the treat, and as he does, tell him "good find!"

and do it again, this time moving the food out further. What we're teaching the dog here is that the "find it" means go and seek out what I just let you sniff! Within 3-4 times you can then hide food behind a chair (with your dog still watching you). Once you see him running out on command and looking, it's time to start hiding the food in another room. Always keep the food on the floor so the dog doesn't learn bad manners and start counter cruising. Jezzie and I have this game down to a science. She graduated to finding toys years ago. I place her in a stay command by the kitchen door, show her the toy I'm hiding, and then go into the living room and hide the toy. I booby trap the room by placing her other toys around on the floor. I then tell her from the living room to find it. She comes racing out, and begins her search. She will look at the various toys on the floor, but knows that she's looking for one in particular. I haven't tricked her for years on this one. It's amazing to me that she can find the exact toy I showed her. And we don't use the same toy for find it all the time. She gets to use her brains as well as her eyes and nose for this fun game.

Fetch: The game of fetch can be one of the most entertaining games for both children and dogs. Fetch must be taught first by an adult, and then supervised with the child while the dog is transferring what he learned. To teach fetch you must first teach sit and give. Once your dog is giving on command then put him on a long lead or retractable leash and throw the toy. Tell him to come, sit and give. By keeping him on a leash he doesn't get the chance to learn the bad habit of running out for a toy and then running around the yard trying to get you to chase him. Don't be in a hurry to take off the leash until you're sure he's understanding the game. The reason I like to teach sit is that a dog running full blast back with a toy can do two things. One, he can knock over a child standing there, and two, he can fly right by you. We taught Jezzie to drop it when playing with children. I always feel comfortable having kids play fetch with her because I know she'll come back, lay down (it's that border collie thing to always want to lay down. It's what she would do if she were herding sheep), and spit out the ball. She then waits in a down until the child picks up the ball, then she's up and ready to go!

Fetch can be a great way to burn off energy for your dog. Once you've trained your dog, and your child can take over, you'll have the best of two worlds. A child that can be part of the care of the dog and a dog that is tired! Remember, a tired dog is a good dog!. Might go the same for kids too!

Tricks: Kids are really good at teaching dogs tricks. They seem to have a knack for seeing something the dog does naturally and putting a word to it. In my Kids Class, the children have to teach their dogs a trick for the final training session. It's always great to see what they come up with. One girl taught her dog to watch her, but put the word statue to it. When she said statue, the dog sat and without blinking or moving a muscle stared at the girl. A smart girl taking something her dog was doing and putting a command to it. Tricks don't have to be complicated or flashy. They can

be as simple as saying shake when your dog puts his paw into your hand. Let your child's imagination go on this one and you'll be pleasantly surprised at what they come up with!

Reading: For the child that is old enough to read, encourage them to read to their dogs. Dogs love to hear our voices. They really like it when we put inflection into it. Reading is such an important part of our children's education, yet often they rebel against it. Having them read a story to their dog may open up that door so they enjoy it. This would be a good time to put the leash on your dog and practice a down stay. Settle the child into his favorite reading place and put the dog into a down next to him. Keep the reading time short, no more than five minutes. Dogs, just like children, can have short attention spans!

Singing: For young children who can't read yet, I encourage them to sing their favorite songs to their dog. My dogs love to hear me sing. I sing to them while I brush them, do their nails, or just cuddle with them. Sometimes as a family we get into "basset howls" where we start to howl and the dogs join in. We laugh the entire time, and everyone enjoys it!

What the human/canine relationship teaches your child

There is no better teacher than a dog to help your child understand fairness, kindness, patience and love. Jake and Kelsey spent alot of time together. She was a wonderfully forgiving teacher. She never yelled at him (or me!), she was never too busy to play a game or cuddle on the floor while he watched cartoons. He could talk to her and she would always listen. He watched her grow old as he grew up, and when he was thirteen years old and she was twelve, she said goodbye to him for the last time. Although it's hard for a child to lose a pet, it's also a life lesson of the process of living and dying. Jake has since trained another basset and will begin showing his third basset, our Gus, in obedience. The world of dogs has been a wonderful place for Jake to practice being a kind person, and I know he'll be all the better for Kelsey's part in his life.

W.O.W. Children and dogs can do very well together under adult supervision and proper education. Dogs should not be considered stuffed toys that the children can handle in any fashion. Given the chance, dogs can be great teachers and best friends for our children. Dogs, as well as children, do not come preprogrammed on how to properly interact with each other. As adults it's our job to help mold their relationship into a safe and harmonious kinship. Remember, your child will imitate your training techniques, so if you are using harsh methods with your dog, your child may very well follow suit.

Kids Class at AllBreed

Fun at the park!

12
A tired dog is a good dog!

You've heard me use that phrase over and over in this book. A lot of my clients do not understand how to properly exercise their dog. Proper exercise can eliminate many behavior problems. Mental exercise can be as tiring as physical, depending on what the dog is doing. I know that when I come home from a visit to a nursing home, my dogs are tired. The physical work they did was minimal, but they did a lot of mental work.

Here are some ideas that perhaps you hadn't thought of to tire out that energetic dog of yours!

Dog Parks: Living in the suburbs of St. Paul, Minnesota, I am fortunate to have a dog park within 8 miles of my home. It is on public park land and has an active user group called R.O.M.P. (Responsible Owners of Mannerly Pets). It is operated on a volunteer basis; the one I go to is very well run. At this park, dogs are allowed to run free off leash. This gives them the opportunity to interact with other canines, socialize with other humans, or if they prefer simply sniff and smell to their hearts content. The park is well used, and rules are respected and followed. There are paths through the field and around the woods that can be walked, or the dogs can play in the large open field. There is a small pond nearby that ROMP is trying to have included in the park so that the dogs that want to can swim. My dogs enjoy it, and it gives them a sense of freedom that we can't have anywhere else. The first fear of anyone who hasn't come to the park is that their dog will run away. Let me tell you, this is doggie heaven, and the dogs that are there keep each other busy. There is no need to go anywhere else. I have set up play dates with my students, letting them know that I'm going out and that anyone who cares to join me may. I typically get 25 or more students to join me. It's gives the ones who are coming for the first time a sense of security that their trainer is there, so all will be well. I remind them that this is the perfect place to practice recalls with their dogs. It's also an opportunity to reward their dogs for checking in. The flip side of having your trainer there is that you will be expected to work as well!

My Gus loves going to the park. When we get there we have to walk 600 feet through the woods to get to the park area. Dogs must be leashed until they get to the designated area. Gus will start to sound his excitement as we walk up, meaning he begins to bark and howl. One day as we came around to the entrance of the park, there was a group of people standing there, staring at us. They took one look at Gus and started to laugh. It seemed they had heard him coming and were sure that Cujo was on the way! After seeing it was only a basset, all fears were extinguished! Gus barks the first five minutes he's there, it never fails. I let him, after all, he's at the dog park. At home we have to curtail his barking in respect to our neighbors. It's nice to have a place where not only is it acceptable, but folks find it entertaining!

I have to say that I also enjoy going. It's a social time for humans as well, as we stand and watch our dogs interact and play. We also chat amiably with each other about our pets. An hour can go by quickly, and the car ride home is always quiet and peaceful as the dogs crash as soon as we pull out of the parking lot.

I know many people who make going to the dog park part of their daily or weekly ritual. From a trainer's point of view, it's a great place to practice obedience. From a behaviorist's point of view I find watching the dogs interact the best classroom I could attend.

Leash Walks: Unless you have a very small dog, or a basset, a walk may not be enough exercise to properly tire out your dog. Strolling with you at a comfortable pace is wonderful for him, but not physically taxing. He will come home happy that he was out, but not overly tired.

Running With Your Dog: Depending on the breed, your dog may be the perfect running companion. Be sure when you're thinking of a dog that you consider what you like to do for relaxation and exercise, as your dog should be able to accompany you. Folks who run with their dogs are getting the best of both worlds, a companion and protector, and in this day and age, it's good to have two for the price of one!

Fetch: For the dog that loves to fetch, this could be the perfect pasttime. I know many dogs who live for the tennis ball to be tossed. If your dog fits into this category, then you have a great way to burn off excess energy and not tire yourself as you do it! Teaching the proper way to play fetch can make for some quality time between dog and owner.

Obedience: Training for obedience can be mildly taxing physically, but tremendously tiring mentally. The hardest part of obedience training is keeping it challenging for both the dog and yourself. I always encourage my students to train their dogs as though they were going into competition, even if they never step one foot in the ring. Many of the obedience competition exercises can be very useful in the home environment, and I show them how to transfer these skills. Not only does this training stimulate the dog, it also ensures that the owner will be interacting with the dog on a daily basis as they practice. After all, it's very boring being a family dog. Nothing to do all day but sleep, eat and occasionally go for walks. Although we all joke about how great our dogs have it, I must say it would get very boring quickly.

Using Natural Instincts: In the dog's perfect world, if he was bred to hunt, he would be able to. If he was bred to herd, he would have sheep living with him. In the real world we don't always have that available for our dogs. But for those that have the interest and time to pursue their dog's natural talents, it can be a lot of fun. Taking a hunting class, even if you've never shot a gun, will give you the opportunity to watch your dog work instinctively. I have friends who have gotten into hunting trials with their dogs who never hunt for recreation. They simply do it for the joy of watching and competing with their dogs.

   Herding trials are another way for dogs to use their natural talents. We are fortunate to have some very good herding trainers in this area. These folks are willing to work with all breeds, but most importantly they are willing to work with novice owners who don't understand the drive their herding dog has, much less how a sheep's brain works! I tried to do a bit of herding with my border collie, Jezzie, but didn't go too far with it. I opted to channel her energy into other areas. There is still a part of me, though, that wishes we had done more of it. When I watched her work the sheep, I could see she knew more about them instinctively than I ever would. I've made myself a promise that my next border collie will teach me to herd!

Tracking is a sport that once learned can be done, simply for the fun of it, anywhere, at just about anytime. This is where a person will walk through a field for up to 300 feet, turning a few times, and at the end dropping an article of theirs, usually a glove. The dog, who is on a harness and 40 feet of line, is brought up to the start, given the scent and told to track. The dog must follow the track and find the article. Here is a sport where your dog can use his nose to his hearts content. My bassets love the sport. Although I love the outdoors, I'm not much for being out in the climate. I'm rather a "fair weather" kind of person.   Here in Minnesota that means I can track about two weeks out of the year, otherwise it would be too wet, too cold, too hot or too windy. This sport is open to any dog that has a nose, which they all do. My breeder is an A.K.C. tracking judge, and she trains classes on tracking. I have seen her work with a number of breeds, including a Scottish Terrier, a Pomeranian, and a variety of terriers. In this sport they get to use their brains, their noses and their bodies.

Go To Ground and racing are favorite sports for the terriers that love to chase vermin into holes or race after their prey. If you have a terrier of any kind, be sure to check out your local breed club, as they often hold fun days where you can bring your dog and have help teaching him the tunnels and rules of racing!

Sight hound clubs also have sports designated to take advantage of their dogs natural instinct to chase by sight. These breeds would include whippets and greyhounds, to name just a few. It's very exciting to watch these dogs run at top speed after their prey of an imitation squirrel tail.

Agility is the chosen sport for those with dogs that love to jump and run. Obedience schools are offering classes for this as it's popularity has soared in the past few years. It is an obstacle course for dogs, including an A-frame that the dogs must go over, tunnels, both open and closed, jumps of various types, a teeter-totter, and a dog walk. It's a timed sport so you are competing with the clock. It's a wonderful confidence builder for dogs who are a bit worried about things. After an hour of class work, your dog is bound to be tired!

Flyball is a sport for the tennis crazy dog. This would be the dog that thinks, eats and dreams about tennis balls! It is a team sport made up of four members. The dogs are required to jump over special flyball jumps as they run toward the box that hold the tennis ball. The must step on the box in order to release the ball, which must be caught as or grabbed as it flys out. The dog must then come back over the jumps and once over the finish line the next dog goes. This is a timed sport, and dogs love it. If you've never been to a flyball match and are considering going to watch, be sure to bring ear plugs. The dogs bark and yip their excitement as they wait for their turn, and it's nonstop. It's perfectly ok for them to do so as it increases their excitement and drive to get the ball. This can be a very physical sport, and the dog needs to be in good shape to partici-pate in it.   Because it requires at least 80 feet of space for the course, not all schools have the space to offer it.

Frisbee competition is also gaining in popularity. This sport combines agility, drive and mental prowess. The dog must decide how fast to go, when to jump, and catch the frisbee, all in a few seconds. This sport is as much fun to watch as it is to train for! Even if you never compete, playing frisbee may be a very good outlet for the right kind of dog.

Swimming is a wonderful way to keep a dog in shape without putting physical stress on the dog's joints. It's also a good way to tire them out! The hard part can be finding a place that is safe and legal for your dog to be off leash. What many folks do is put their dogs on long 50' leads and take them into the water. That way the dog is still legally leashed, but able to enjoy a swim.

Visiting Nursing homes and hospitals can be very rewarding for both you and your dog. At AllBreed we have a Canine Cheer Club where we visit the local nursing homes. In order to be part of the club, your dog must have the Canine Good Citizen title, which we'll talk about next. If your dog enjoys social outings, this is a sure fit!

Canine Good Citizen title is a wonderful thing to put on the family dog. It is supported by the American Kennel Club. This title proves to the community that you have a well mannered, respected and cared for pet. The program encourages both purebred and mixed breed dogs to participate. The dog must have written proof of rabies vaccination and a copy of the city license (tags are not sufficient). The ten tests are as follows: 1) accepting a friendly stranger, 2) sitting politely for petting, 3) appearance and grooming, 4) walking on a loose leash, 5) walking through a crowd, 6) sit and down on command and staying in place, 7) coming when called, 8) reaction to another dog, 9) reactions to distractions, and 10) supervised separation. The dog must pass all ten tests to receive the certificate. For the dog that has basic training, these tests may seem simple. I'm always happy to tell my students that they should have no problem passing these tests. It shows that they have worked with their dogs. The dog that has had no training would not be able to pass.

I offer Canine Good Citizen classes, as do a few other schools. The class includes training for the tests, and the final week is the evaluation. CGC tests are often included in fun matches held at local dog clubs or at licensed dog shows.

Take your dog with you whenever you can. Keeping the dog busy will tire him out and make him a calmer housemate. Take the dog with you when you watch your children play sports. Include them on a weekend trip to Grandma's house. Remember, these dogs are companions as well as canines. The more time they spend with us, the calmer they are socially.

So be creative in how you spend time with your dog. Your individual interests can include your four footed friend. Dr. Kate An Hunter owns a horse, and whenever she goes out her dog comes along. Another friend of mine roller blades with his husky, who will pull him up the hills! All the more reason to be sure that the dog you want fits your lifestyle as well as your heart!

W.O.W. Unchanneled energy in a dog can create havoc in the family setting. Ugly behaviors can arise, including barking, chewing or wild excitement. As owners, it's our job to find ways to burn off our dogs energy in an acceptable and enjoyable manner for both dog and human. Using our dogs natural instincts can help shape the type of exercise we have them do. Enjoy your dog, include him in your own recreational activities and you'll have a calmer and more bonded dog.

13
Owning multiple dogs

Making the decision to add another dog takes as much thought and homework as getting your first puppy. Although you may have decided to get the same breed of puppy, you now have your existing dog to take into consideration.

Gender is now an important consideration, wherein the sex of your new puppy may be dependent on your existing dog. If your existing dog is a neutered male, you can choose between a male or female, as we find that neutered males get along well with either for a housemate. If you have a female, you should consider gettting a male, as two females in the house do not always get along. This is not to say that there aren't folks out there that have two females who are wonderful together. My two old girls, Dara and Kelsey, lived together for 12 years without so much as a growl between them. Typically, though, when we have housemates that aren't getting along, it's two females. Remember, females can be more moody, less apt to forgive and, with some breeds, will fight to the death.

The tricky thing about adding another dog is that you have to know your existing dog's personality very well. If your dog doesn't get along with or enjoy the company of other dogs, adding a puppy isn't the answer to his problem. People make the mistake of thinking that if they bring in a puppy, their existing dog will learn how to accept all other dogs. This won't happen. It may be that your existing dog accepts the new puppy after a time, but he will still have problems with outside dogs. Don't bring a new puppy in hoping to fix your existing dogs problems.

You also have to look for temperament blends.

If you know that senior dog is very dominant, do your best to find a more middle of the road puppy. Blending canine personalities is a bit like a marriage. If you get two strong personalities, there is bound to be friction.

Owning more than one dog is a challenge as much as it is a reward. When you have two or more dogs, you have a dog pack. The social structure within the dog pack is something a human cannot control. As hard as it may seem to us, age does not dictate hierarchy in a dog pack. We cannot tell the young adolescent puppy to stand behind the older dog in pack order. They will decide between themselves who will take the place as leader. Although they have their own set hierarchy, always remember that the humans hold the highest positions, and the dogs take the rest.

DON'T BRING IN A NEW DOG IF:
* If you have a dog that is older, over ten, or one that has some medical issues, it may not be the time to bring in a new dog. So often I have clients who, because they don't want to be without a dog when Senior passes bring in a young, energetic puppy. We do this so that our own sorrow will be softened, but what often ends up happening is that our Senior dog now has to handle new stresses. If Senior is medically impaired he may find the antics of a young puppy not only aggravating, but painful as well. Think about your older dogs well being before bringing in a pup. Another consideration is that when the old dog passes, Junior is left alone. He will go through a mourning period, and you may end up purchasing yet another dog to fill Junior's void. Best to wait and give your older dog all the attention and medical care you can. Soon enough there will be a place for a puppy.
* If the dog you have now isn't trained to where you have comfortable control, you may want to wait. Training two dogs at the same time is a challenge even the best dog trainer would have trouble with. If your dog has behavior issues going on, for example, dog aggression, fear or separation anxiety, take care of these issues before you bring in Junior. Dogs learn from each other, and bad behaviors can be passed from one dog to another, so instead of having one dog

barking you now have two. Don't make the mistake of thinking that having another dog will make Senior happier and calmer. If he has behavior issues going on, it could make them worse.

Introducing a new puppy

When bringing a puppy into a household with an existing dog, there are some courtesies we should extend to our senior canine. If you have an adult dog between the ages of 2-8, bringing in a new puppy will take some adjustment on their part. They are used to having you all to themselves, so care must be taken that as you spread out your attention, you're not short changing the senior dog. Continue to give your senior dog those special walks with just the two of you, and feel free to put the puppy away in his crate for a nap so Senior can rest comfortably in his favorite place unterrupted for a while.

Always remember that you are the boss. Expect some canine interaction between the two as the adult teaches the puppy what the rules are in his house. Teeth may be flashed, a puppy may be snapped at or knocked over. These are appropriate ways for your senior dog to communicate to the puppy. What isn't appropriate is when blood is shed. You know your senior dog best, so don't take the wait and see approach. Be protactive, but not overly protective of the puppy. Being a fair leader means that you stop things before they get out of hand.

Don't expect your senior dog to immediately love and bond with the new puppy. Senior will probably tolerate many obnoxious behaviors by the pup. Clients sometimes tell me they wish Senior would put Junior in his place. Senior's temperment will play a large role in how he responds to the puppy. As the puppy grows and hormones begin to navigate the puppy's behavior, you will find that your senior dog will be less tolerant There may be small scuffles over toys and food as the dogs realign their pack order with each other. Be prepared that small interactions are perfectly ok, but big ones need your intervention.

Be it an adult or puppy being introduced to the family, I always encourage clients to make the initial meeting on neutral ground. That could be the neighbor's yard or the park or even out in the street. This way Senior doesn't think he has to defend his territory from the newcomer. Once they're getting along nicely on the neutral ground, move them to your front yard. Then go to the back yard, and make the inside of the house the last stop.

If your Senior dog is showing signs of serious aggression towards the puppy, put the puppy in his crate or an exercise pen so the adult dog can smell him without the puppy jumping in his face. We often bring a Board and Train dog into our house for a few hours of in-home training. Maybee, the basset, is always introduced to the new dog in this fashion. It gives her time to evaluate the situation, and see the new dog without feeling threatened.

Be sure that your new puppy has his own space, and that he isn't trying to take over the senior's kennel. By crate training your puppy from day one, you will ensure that he has a clear understanding of his place.

Introducing an adult dog

If you are adopting an older dog, one six months or older, then some other rules will come into play.

Introduce the two dogs in the same manner as the puppy, by having them meet on neutral ground and slowly progressing into the senior dog's territory.

Keep a leash on each dog so that if a scuffle starts, you can end it safely by grabbing the leash and not the dogs. Always remember, never, never put your hands into a dog fight. You will end up getting bit. Using a loud voice, stomping on the floor, or tossing water or a jacket at the two is a safer way to interrupt the behavior. I have known many a good hearted owner who was bitten by his own dog because he tried to physically interfere with a fight.

Keep the rules the same for the new dog as you have for the senior dog. Don't make exceptions for behavior. Your senior dog will not understand why junior gets to lay on the couch when he never has been able to. Adult dogs will immediately start working on dominance between the two of them. These issues can sometimes be taken care of before we even know they're happening. It will be a continual test between the two for weeks. I will ask clients who drinks first out of the water bowl, who goes out the door first, as we try to establish who is leader in their dog pack. Many times they tell me it changes from day to day, which means the two of them haven't really settled it yet. Our part in this is to treat the two equally until we are absolutely sure who is the alpha. Without meaning to we can add a lot of stress between the two by feeling sorry for the submissive dog and feeding him first or giving him attention first. Remember, the alpha dog gets everything from us first. This is the most basic rule of the pack.

As an owner of multiple dogs myself, I spend a lot of time ensuring that each dog keeps his individuality. I do this by taking time to train, play or socialize with them one-on-one. My dogs are a great pack together. They enjoy playing with each other, sleeping by each other and co-existing with each other. But they still need me for leadership, food and fun. If you're under the impression that by owning two or more dogs your work will be less, think again. As I stated earlier, dogs that aren't bonded with their human, but are bonded with the other dog, have no need to please or listen to their owners. They have each other and certainly don't need you. Remember that for every dog you own, you increase the amount of work, time and money that you must invest in order to have a well balanced dog.

Owning multiple dogs also means you must respect their differences. What worked to train Senior may not work very well for Junior. Senior may have been a little more hard headed and Junior may be very soft. When I train my three dogs I have to constantly shift gears, as each one has their own approach to learning. You must be flexible if you own multiple dogs!

As stated in the chapter "Saying No," when you have more than one dog you need to have an individual No word for each dog. This will differentiate the interrupter so that the intended dog gets the message and the other isn't bothered by it. At my house No is the universal word that everyone is in trouble! On the other hand, if I say "can" to Maybee, she responds while the others just ignore it. Keep that in mind if you're thinking of using any of those sound oriented correction collars. Some bark collars have a loud noise which is fine except the other dog can hear it and is corrected for doing nothing. Using motion sensors to catch a thief at the garbage can will alert you to the crime, but the dog that isn't doing it will also hear the noise and perhaps be affected.

You must also be more in tune with pack mentality. As stated earlier, your dogs are now a canine pack of two or more. They will constantly be watching and testing each other to see if there has been a change or a weakness where they can move up in their position. These behaviors can be subtle or excessive. Some can be ignored, others cannot. You, as the leader, must make the decision as to when you should intercede or simply let them work it out.

Personally, I love owning multiple dogs. I enjoy watching the canine interaction that goes on every day between the three of them. When I watch T.V. and opt to sit on the floor, I'm guaranteed three warm bodies around me! Each dog has their own place in my heart, and my family's as well. These are not just dogs to us, they are family. How did I come up with this many dogs? Michael tells everyone who asks that question, that "each time she wanted another baby, I bought her a dog!" I always wanted a large family, I just never thought it would be with canines rather than children!

★ W.O.W. If you have more than one dog you have a canine pack. It's important that you are aware of canine behaviors and understand how they are communicating to each other. When you own more than one dog you absolutely must be the leader in the house. I have seen dogs fight with each other for the alpha role because the humans weren't doing their job.

Have fun and laugh together

14
Final Words of Wisdom

There is so much more to say about our canine friends, but only so much time to write and read about them. What I hope I've left you with is a better understanding of what your dog is telling you and what you may be inadvertently telling them. Always remember that every dog has his own individual approach to life, learning and love! Never compare them with past dogs that you may have owned or known. Many folks have been disappointed when comparing their dog to that infamous "dog from their childhood." Time has a way of altering our memories, and we may have forgotten certain things not so wonderful about that dog. This does not mean you ever forget the dogs that have touched your life. I have a place for each and every one I have lived with and loved, and I know I have room for more!

When you live with a canine you receive unconditional love. They will be there for you when you're sad, when you're happy or when you're lonely. They never ask for much except a walk around the park, a good bowl of dog food and an old-fashioned belly rub now and then. Of course, from reading this book you know they need much more in order to be acceptable citizens in this complex world we call society. Never underestimate the power of the canine/human bond. Our influence over these dogs shows itself in how they communicate with others and us. Don't forget that they have a very strong sense of hearing, taste, smell and sight. They also have an extra sense that we humans call the sixth sense. I hear stories of it all the time. My own story is from a recent two week stint at my parent's house sitting and watching their five month old puppy, Reggie. I left Jezzie, my border collie at home and had been at the my folks for four days. I woke up Tuesday morning about 2:00 a.m., with this really heavy feeling of missing my Jezzie. It was a physical sadness that had been intense enough to wake me up. I roamed around the house for a bit, and decided then and there that come morning I was going to go get her and have her stay with me. I was then able to go back to sleep. The next morning I called over to my house and before I could tell Michael my intentions he said, "you know, you should come and get Jezzie. She really misses you. Last night about 2:00 a.m. she was up and roaming around the room, and then she finally settled back down." I think we were linked that morning and that she "heard" me decide to come and get her the next day. Can dogs pick up on our thoughts? I was told from day one during obedience competition to visualize my dog and myself doing well, and to never think "don't lay down" during the sit stay, as the dog will "hear" or perhaps "see" the word down and more than likely they would drop. I'm sure if you take the time to think about it, you will think of your own experiences where your dog just seemed to know what you wanted before you told him. On this same line I often wonder if we "imprint" our attitudes about dogs into them. By this I mean if we constantly think they're bad dogs, and are always saying, "he's so naughty, he's untrainable, etc." might we be sending them the wrong message? It's not unlike the thought that if a child is constantly told how bad he is, instead of how good he is, that he will see himself as bad. I know you probably think I'm stretching here a bit, as children are certainly not dogs. But remember, canines are extremely sensitive to their environment. A one-time incident can stay with them for life. When Jezzie was one year old, Michael took her to a herding clinic. They used a method where they shook out towels at the dogs to make them move in certain directions. It really frightened Jezzie. To this day, nine and one half years later, if I start to fold clothes of any kind, and have to shake them out first, she will dart out of the room. The incident happened long ago, and only once, but she never forgot it. I may have inadvertently encouraged the fear because I've always known how she would react, and certainly, every time I fold clothes I think "where is Jezzie, I don't want to shake this around her." Can she hear me think that? Maybe, then again, maybe not. But in the world of the canine, who's to say what they do and don't "hear".

Lastly, and most importantly, have fun with your dog. If you're not enjoying each other, your relationship can be long and tedious. In many of my classes I encourage students to teach their dogs a trick as part of the graduation night. They have ten weeks to work on something silly and fun. The trick can be something the dog does naturally and are able to put a word to. Some like the challenge of doing more complicated tricks. It's a personal preference, but one that has the same outcome. The students end up laughing with their dogs as they try to figure out ways to make them hold that biscuit on their nose or roll over. Laughter is the best medicine in dog training. It ensures that neither dog nor student are getting too serious about something that should be fun as well as educational. This winter I plan on having a "silly picture" contest where students can enter photographs that have both themselves and their dogs just hanging loose. When we took the picture of Jezzie and me (where I pretended to grab her around her neck) we were both having a great time. Afterwards she raced around the park looking over her shoulder as if to say "you are the best!".

For some, fun is walking through the park, or sitting on the couch together eating popcorn and watching a movie. Whatever your preference, as long as both you and the dog are smiling, you've found the magic formula.

So as you can see, solving the canine puzzle isn't as hard as you may have thought. No matter the size, color or shape, they all have dog instincts and will respond as one. Always remember they are canines, not humans, and life will go well for you both. Love them, spoil them, but give them the structure and understanding that they require to live in a human/canine pack.

Respect your dog and he will respect you. Listen and see what your dog is telling you as he is always communicating with you. I know that I'm here today writing this book because of the things my first dog, Kelsey, taught me. If I hadn't listened to her, I would have never tried to find a different approach to dog training. Your dog, too, has messages he wants you to have. Listen with your heart, and may you both enjoy a long, harmonious life together.

Debra Schneider
October, 1999

ORDER FORM

To order more copies of <u>Seeing Eye to Eye, Solving the Canine Puzzle:</u>

Email orders: HYPERLINK mail to:Aobedience@aol.com

Postal Orders: AllBreed Obedience
                2201 Ventura Drive, Woodlbury, MN 55125
Name:_____
Address:_____
City:_____ State_____Zip Code_____

For confirmation of receipt of order:
Phone number:_____ email address_____

Number of Copies Requested _____ @ $16.95 per copy

Sales Tax: Please add 6.5% for books shipped to a Minnesota addresses.

Shipping Charge: U.S.: $4.00, first book, $2.00 each additional book.
            International: $9.00, first book, $5.00 each additional book

Total $_____

Payment: ☐ Check   ☐ Credit Card
            ☐ Visa   ☐ MasterCard   ☐ Discover

Card Number:_____
Name on Card:_____ Exp. Date_____

Please send me more FREE information on:
☐ Upcoming Books   ☐ Speaking Seminars   ☐ Newsletter List

☐ Consulting   ☐ Class Schedules   ☐ Board & Train

About the Author:

Debra Schneider has always had a dog at her side. In 1985 she brought a basset hound by the name of Kelsey into her life. Kelsey would change her life, as well as her career focus. Between 1988 and 1991, Schneider was involved in many different activities and organizations, including teaching obedience for a Community Education group, working with children and their dogs in the Ramsey County 4-H Club, started her private training sessions in homes and also pioneered the first Puppy Kindergarten class for the 3M Obedience Club. In 1991 Schneider and a partner opened Top Dog Training Academy in Hudson, Wisconsin. In 1996 she left the partnership to open her own school in Woodbury, Minnesota, ALLBREED OBEDIENCE AND BEHAVIORAL SCHOOL FOR DOGS. This business includes not only obedience at the Puppy Kindergarten, Beginner and Advanced levels, but also behavioral training, as it was clear to Schneider after years of working with the family dogs, that obedience was not the only answer to a harmonious relationship between humans and canines. She also includes other classes of interest, those being tracking, agility, a Canine Good Citizen Class, and clicker classes. She recognized the need for children to be part of the training process of the family dog, and has developed a Kids Beginner class, which is very unique, educational as well as fun for both the kids participating and the adults supervising. Throughout the year she offers seminars on various dog training and behavior issues. During these years and to present she is deeply involved and dedicated to helping dogs, and volunteers with various animal shelters and rescue groups. She currently shares her life with three dogs, and co-owns one. She actively competes with all her dogs at various dogs sports, and does therapy visits with her dogs.

Being a professional dog trainer had been a second job for many years for Schneider, who had worked at 3M for 16 years. In 1996 she opted to make a big move and leave the world of business to "go to the dogs" full time. She has never regretted her decision. The fascinating world of the human/canine relationship makes for a rewarding and challenging profession, one she feels fortunate to be part of! By writing her book, *Seeing Eye to Eye With Your Dog,* she hopes to help folks with the every day challenges of owning a dog by helping them see through the dog's eyes.

We hope you enjoyed this book. Look for the second of the *Seeing Eye to Eye* series, *Dog vs. Training*, coming out in the summer of 2000.

This second book will cover in detail the training approaches Debra has defined throughout her career of working with hundreds of dogs and students.

The third in the series, *What's a Dog to Do?*, will be out in the winter of 2001. It will be the last of *Seeing Eye to Eye* series and will talk about what to do with a dog beyond the training years.

AllBreed Obedience & Behavioral School for Dogs
2201 Ventura Drive
Woodbury, MN 55125
651-704-9785

Debra and Michael Schneider, owners/trainers

Please visit our website: www.Allbreedobedience.com

Notes:

Notes:

Notes:

Notes: